Prophetic Voices in an Age of Upheaval

PROPHETIC VOICES IN AN AGE OF UPHEAVAL

Meditations on the Minor Prophets

Garry E. Milley

CLEMENTS PUBLISHING
Toronto, Ontario

Prophetic Voices in an Age of Upheaval

This edition published 2004 by
Clements Publishing
213-6021 Yonge Street
Toronto, Ontario
M2M 3W2 Canada
www.clementspublishing.com

National Library of Canada Cataloguing in Publication Data

Milley, Garry E.

Prophetic voices in an age of upheaval:
meditations on the minor prophets / Garry E. Milley.

Includes some material first published in The lion roars.
ISBN 1-894667-42-5

1. Bible. O.T. Minor Prophets--Meditations. I. Milley,
Garry E. Lion roars. II. Title.

BS1560.M545 2004 224'.9 C2004-900886-2

Contents

Foreword

Thousands have meditated upon the message of the Minor Prophets since *The Lion Roars* was first published in 1988. I have found this book in theological colleges around the world and have recommended it to many classes of students as I have taught in these institutions. The book has been relevant in all cultural settings and has addressed the issues of the times.

Its revision under the title, *Prophetic Voices in an Age of Upheaval* is very timely. Both themes, upheaval in the world and the prophetic voice of the church have become predominant in the last decade. The first is evidenced in the events that have happened since the book first appeared. Sept. 11/2001 stunned the world; the nations of the world are at war with terrorism; the Middle East still seethes with turmoil and tension; and cracks appear in Western alliances that seemed to be unbreakable. Many of the nations at the center of today's upheavals are the same as those of the prophets' times.

The second theme, the prophetic voice, has been at the forefront of faith groups all around the world during the last decade. The church, in its clamor to be relevant, is returning to the tried and proven way of the prophets. They are entering the courts of God, examining the messages of Hosea, Amos and Micah and finding them up with the times. They are following in the tradition of the great ninth century prophet, Elijah, and are becoming "troublers" to the conscience of their nations. The Lion Roars as loudly in the second issue of Milley's book as in the first. He does not tone down his passion that the last word must be God's word. The messages of the prophets are not opinions, but absolutes: not trivial, but critical; not parochial but universal.

The prophetic voice is not only meant for the nations but also for the people of God. Any church that applies the principles found within this book will be revolutionized. The call to holiness, repentance, justice, mercy and commitment is clearly heard in the plea of the prophets and should resound in the prophetic voice of the church today. As with the first edition, the second is meant for church leaders and congregations alike, for the prophetic voice is a divine blend of a multitude of voices in a multitude of languages calling a multitude of nations back to God. *Prophetic Voices in an Age of Upheaval* inspires us all to be part of that voice.

Dr. Carl F. Verge

PREFACE

This small volume is intended for a general audience. It is not meant to be a critical introduction to, or a commentary on, the Minor Prophets. Those interested in a more scholarly approach may find help in the several good textbooks included in the bibliography. My purpose in writing is pastoral and practical. I have not said the last word and I urge all who read to improve upon it. I have attempted to make the message of the prophets plain so as to exhort Christians in the life of discipleship. After all, Scripture was given to lead us to Christ and then to Christ-likeness. Only my readers will know if I have succeeded.

The chapters in this book were originally published in a modified form in *Good Tidings*, the official publication of the Pentecostal Assemblies of Newfoundland. I express my thanks to my good friend the Reverend Roy D. King, former General Superintendent of the Pentecostal Assemblies of Newfoundland and editor of *Good Tidings*, for permission to reissue the series of articles in its present form.

I am grateful to God for spiritual strength and grace during the writing of the book, which took place within a very busy schedule of preaching and teaching both at, what is now Master's College and Seminary and Tyndale University College and Seminary.

No book, however modest the effort, is done alone. Many people have directly and indirectly helped in this endeavor. My interest in writing on the prophets was first stimulated in seminary during a course with Dr. Donald A. Leggett, a professor with a deep passion for the Christian faith. Alvin W. Winsor, at our Smitty's conferences, reaffirmed my intent to write for the layperson and not for the theological student. He, along with Douglas James and John W. Stephenson, read the entire manuscript and gave many helpful suggestions. I express thanks to them all. They share in the strengths of the book. I alone bear the weaknesses. I express appreciation to Dr. Carl Verge, former President of Eastern Pentecostal Bible College, now Master's College and Seminary, for kindly agreeing to write the foreword. I wish to thank Erika D. Milley for typing the manuscript and Rob Clements for his helpful suggestions.

Lastly, I wish to thank my wife, Christine, for her patience. The extra hours away from her and our delightful children, Erika, Andrew and Philip, placed an additional burden on her shoulders. She would have been justified in complaining that, this year, I spent more time with the prophets than with her. She didn't. To her this book is affectionately dedicated.

Garry E. Milley
Master's College & Seminary, Toronto

Introduction

Christians need to rediscover the Hebrew Scriptures. Contained within its pages is a word which the Lord wants his church to hear. In it is untold wealth for the spiritual life of God's people. As the neglect of it has brought spiritual poverty, so its rediscovery will bring spiritual riches.

The church has long recognized the value of the historical narratives for examples of holy lives and God's gracious providence. Also, the Psalms have provided the Christian church with both songs and prayers for two millennia. However, for most of us, the Old Testament is still unexplored and uncharted territory.

There are several reasons why this is so. Some Christians see the Old Testament only as the Jewish background for the New Testament. Since the New is the completion of the Old and gives the proper perspective on the Old, some think it is of limited significance for the Christian. While it is true that the Old Testament does not have the same significance for the church as the New Testament, it is also true that the New Testament cannot be properly understood without knowledge of the Old Testament.

Some Christians have drawn a false separation between the two testaments. They suppose that God saved his people in the

Old Testament by the law but that now in the age of grace God saves us by faith. The fact of the matter is that God has had only one means of salvation. Paul in Galatians and Romans makes it crystal-clear that God saved by faith in all ages. It is this truth of salvation by faith that makes both testaments one book. We may say that under the Old Covenant God's people were saved by faith in the blood of him who was to come, symbolized by the blood of the sacrifices. Under the New Covenant God's people are saved by faith in the blood of him who has come, symbolized in the Holy Communion.

The Old Testament contains many ethical commands, but it is more than a book of laws. Jesus considered the Old Testament to be the Word of God. It was the only Bible he knew. The Old Testament was the only Scripture the first generation of Christians had, for they lived before the New Testament was written. In the Old Testament God revealed himself and proclaimed the coming Messiah through whom salvation was to come. Through it God spoke his Word to his people, giving them meaningful direction and encouragement in difficult times. By it generations of believers have been spiritually nurtured as they have meditated upon its pages. The early Christians did not throw away the Old Testament after the New was written. Instead, they appended the New to the Old to make one Bible. To neglect the Old Testament is to miss the full message God wishes his people to hear.

The Old Testament has been neglected by the church. This is especially true of the prophets. The prophets have long been seen, and rightly so, as the foretellers of the coming of our Lord Jesus Christ. The prophets knew a lot more than we give them credit for (cf. 1 Peter 1:10-12). But all too often they have been the hobby of interpreters who see in them every minute detail of tomorrow's newspaper headlines and more. The prophets do contain much eschatological material. There are predictive elements in their message about the future of human history. However, the prophets were not so much foretellers as *forthtellers* of God's Word to a contemporary situation. They were powerful preachers whose messages were relevant to their times. Their messages need to be rediscovered in ours.

NOTE TO READERS

This book is not meant to be read at one sitting. Maximum benefit will come by reading the chapters only after each respective Old Testament book has first been prayerfully read. The questions for reflection at the end of each chapter may be answered during group study or in a notebook, as the reader desires. After each chapter, the biblical book should be reread.

The meditations expressed in this book are not inspired. This is not the final word on the Minor Prophets. Only the Bible has the honour of being final truth. In this book the writer has been thinking about truth, and the truth must rule the thoughts. If in some way these meditations help the reader to hear the Word of our Lord a little clearer, the writer has been amply rewarded.

CHAPTER 1

HOSEA

The Tender-Hearted Prophet

> The Lord said to me, "Go, show your love to your wife again, though she is loved by another and is an adulteress. Love her as the Lord loves the Israelites, though they turn to other gods and love the sacred raisin-cakes."
>
> So I bought her for fifteen shekels of silver and about a homer and a lethek of barley. Then I told her, "You are to live with me many days; you must not be a prostitute or be intimate with any man, and I will live with you" (3:1-3).

To say the Old Testament prophets were preachers of law but not grace is to be very wide of the mark. Our God is a God of loving-kindness. He is a gracious God. And nowhere is this truth of his character more evident than in the book of Hosea, the tender-hearted prophet of grace.

Hosea ministered to the people of the Northern Kingdom of Israel during years of social collapse (750-725 B.C.). The nation was on the brink of disaster nationally and in an atrocious condition spiritually. God, in mercy, sent his messenger Hosea to warn his people of the inevitable results of their sin. Eventually the people fell into captivity to the Assyrians because they did not heed the prophet's call for repentance.

HOSEA AND UNFAITHFUL GOMER (1-3)

Hosea preaches with the passionate soul of a poet. He is emotionally involved in his ministry. His message is rather complex, following no apparent logical or chronological order since he is speaking from his heart more than his head. However, two basic divisions are evident. Chapters 1-3 relate the unusual story of his marriage, while chapters 4-14 are a series of prophetic speeches containing warnings and promises.

The prophet was ordered by God to marry a woman who would later prove unfaithful to him. Hosea's wife, Gomer, became involved in the sexual excesses of Baal and Ashtaroth worship. (It is interesting to note that the Hebrew words for *holy woman* and *prostitute* are very similar.) She may have become a sacred prostitute at a shrine associated with this pagan cult, but it is also possible that she merely became a call girl. At any rate, we are safe in saying she was a person of dubious character quite unlike that which we would expect in a prophet's wife.

> When the Lord began to speak through Hosea, the Lord said to him, "Go, take yourself an adulterous wife and children of unfaithfulness, because the land is guilty of the vilest adultery in departing from the Lord." So he married Gomer daughter of Diblaim, and she conceived and bore him a son (1:2-3).

Hosea's marriage was both actual and symbolic. It illustrated the broken relationship between God and Israel. Just as Gomer left her husband to follow a life of sexual excess and perversion, Israel had committed spiritual adultery by disregarding the ways of God to associate with idols.

The marriage of Gomer and Hosea was a happy and fruitful one in the beginning at least. Gomer eventually has three children, one by Hosea and, apparently, two by someone else. The first child was named Jezreel, which means "God will scatter," referring to the coming judgment of God upon the nation. The second child, a daughter, was named Lo-ruhamah, meaning "Unloved or unpitied." The name of the third child, a son, was Lo-ammi, which means "Not my people."

It's possible these names may not have been their birth names but labels given later in life. It isn't difficult to imagine the trauma of growing up with a name like "Unloved." It's not the kind of name parents give a newborn baby. However, the names of the children describe in clear terms what sin does to a relationship between God and his people. For the prophet, religion was a matter of personal relationship with God, and sin destroyed the very essence of that relationship. Hosea's marriage was a dramatic object lesson to Israel, not only in that his love for Gomer was rejected, as God's love for Israel was, but also, like God, his love was convicting, convincing and conquering.

Hosea was not a hopeless romantic. He did not behave like an enamoured fan with a neurotic fixation for a movie star. Neither was he a mere puppet on a string performing a play for the people. His was a real marriage "on the rocks." Yet Hosea loved Gomer and remained faithful to her, even when she continued in unfaithfulness. The prophet did not divorce her. Hosea did not seek a way out of the relationship, as many of our contemporaries would have done.

It appears from the story that after Gomer had her fling in the world of sensual indulgence she may have lost her initial physical beauty. A life of sin can age a person and Hosea's wife began to show it. We find her in chapter three being auctioned off as a common work servant. She was harem quality no more. She had been used and abused to such an extent that her price was that of a field slave. Apparently she was not worth much in the end. Yet Hosea paid the asking price and bought back his own wife out of the slave market. It is a touching and moving story. Chapter three of Hosea has even been called the greatest chapter in the Old Testament because it illustrates the glorious truth that we are bought by Christ out of the slave market of sin.

GOD AND UNFAITHFUL ISRAEL (4-14)

Chapters 4-14 record Hosea's prophetic oracles, including warnings and promises. God, through the prophet, makes at least seven specific charges against Israel: the people lack knowledge and this was destroying them (4:6); they are full of such arrogance that it caused them to stumble (5:5); their presumption of unending grace resulted in a shallow repentance that was sporadic and momentary (6:3-4); they are guilty of assimilating the ways of the world and are none the wiser for doing so (7:8-9); they are deep in depravity and corrupt (9:9); they have turned away from God and are backslidden (11:7); and they are involved in idolatry (13:2). Besides this, it appears that they were breaking almost all of the Ten Commandments (4:2).

GOD'S LOVE IS CONVICTING

That is quite a list of sins and it takes up ten chapters of the book! Obviously unconfessed sin is deadly serious and Hosea sees "a vulture over the house of the Lord" (8:1 RSV). It is a dramatic warning. God's people must not abuse his grace or presume that his love means unending tolerance of our sin. We must realize that the love of the Lord is a deeply convicting love. Nothing highlights our unfaithfulness to God like his unfailing love. On the night Peter betrayed our Lord, it was the look in the eyes of

Jesus that convicted Peter so much that he wept tears of repentance (Luke 22). All it took was one look at God and the prophet Isaiah was terrified by his own utter sinfulness (Isaiah 6). God's love penetrates into the deepest parts of our personality. It reached into the hidden places of our lives.

God will never turn a blind eye to our sin as if he had a "boys will be boys" attitude. God cannot pretend that our sin doesn't matter to him. Sin grieves the heart of God for it destroys his fellowship with his people. The yearning love of God cannot but speak out against that which hurts and destroys. That is why God often takes a hard line against sin. God takes his love relationship with us seriously. The chastisement of God is love inflamed. The warnings that come through the lips of the prophet come from the heart of God who hates sin yet is willing to go to great lengths to restore the relationship with his people.

GOD'S LOVE IS CONVINCING

The story is not a fairy tale, and there is no "living happily ever after" here. Even after Gomer was purchased by her husband and brought home away from her sinful environment, things were not always smooth. There was no instant perfection here. Redeemed people still have the pollution of sin remaining even after the guilt of sin is gone. But there is gradual and definite victory as our wills are shaped and formed according to the will of the lover of our souls.

> "She said, 'I will go after my lovers, who give me my food and my water, my wool and my linen, my oil and my drink.' Therefore I will block her path with thornbushes; I will wall her in . . . . She has not acknowledged that I was the one who gave her the grain, the new wine and oil, who lavished on her the silver and gold—which they used for Baal" (2:5-8).

Hosea discovered that he had to "block her path with thornbushes" and to "wall her in" so that Gomer would not follow that proneness to wander. He took pains to convince her that he was the one who was responsible for her welfare. One wonders, if when she was down and out, whether or not Hosea sent her secretly those things mentioned in chapter 2:5. Hosea cared for her even in her fallen state. Apparently, Gomer misunderstood the source of blessing. She thought the good things of life came from her lovers when, all the time, it came from Hosea.

Like so many of God's people, she needed to be convinced of his love. In order to do that, the prophet decided to take away those things for which she yearned. The process of restoration may be very painful, both for the sinner and for God. However, he always stands ready and willing to forgive the truly repentant heart of each and every sinner, and sometimes God has to reduce us to nothing so that we may see that all our blessings find their source in him.

We tend to give credit for our blessings to many things. Sometimes we give credit to our education, our upbringing or our business experience. But all good and perfect gifts come from God, and he alone deserves worship and praise. Hosea says in chapter 2:14, "Therefore I am now going to allure her; I will lead her into the desert and speak tenderly to her." God seeks to convince his people of his love. If we are unconvinced about his love for us, we can never love him as he desires. And, neither can we serve him as he desire if we are unsure of his love for us.

GOD'S LOVE IS CONQUERING

The predominance of prophetic warnings in chapters 4-14 indicates the seriousness of sin both for the individual and for the nation. Sin affects, not just our personal inner lives but our society as a whole. Proverbs 14:34 says, "Righteous exalts a nation but sin is a reproach to any people." However, though Israel eventually was led captive, the book does not end in despair. Love covers a multitude of sins. Just as Hosea's love was triumphant over the sin of Gomer, God's love will conquer in the end. Paul, in Romans 9: 25f., quotes Hosea optimistically in reference to a great ingathering in the last days, when "all Israel shall be saved" (11:26).

LEARNING FROM HOSEA

There are lessons for the church here. If we respond to his love, if we repent and surrender our wills to him, we can enjoy the wonderful blessings of a covenant relationship with God.

As we face the uncertain future, let us surrender to the conquering love of God. Let us not reject it by playing the harlot with the world, the flesh and the devil. If we are pure, let us stay pure. If we are like Gomer, let us return to God, who is gracious and forgiving.

> "Come, let us return to the Lord. He has torn us to pieces but he will heal us; he has injured us but he will bind our wounds . . . .
>
> Let us acknowledge the Lord; let us press on to acknowledge him. As surely as the sun rises, he will appear; he will come to us like the winter rains, like the spring rains that water the earth" (6:1-3).

This is a day of great blessing for many parts of the church. God is pouring out his Spirit as never before. Many congregations that began in storefronts and rented schools now have become large mega-churches. When we compare our present status with our humble beginnings, it is easy to feel a sense of pride. However, let us not forget that it is God who is our source, not our education, attractive churches or our evident success in the eyes of the religious world. Let us give glory to God, who has redeemed us by his precious blood, worthless as we are, from the slave market of sin.

We do not know how this story ended. The biographical information about the prophet and his wife is told to us so that we may understand the greatness of God's character, the nature of his love for us and the extent to which he will go to reclaim his own. No one knows how many "ups and downs" Hosea and Gomer experienced throughout their marriage. All our questions cannot be answered. We do know that the way Gomer treated Hosea is the way we often treat God. Yet, how wonderful to know that the way Hosea treated Gomer is the way God treats us.

QUESTIONS FOR REFLECTION

1. What was the significance of the names of the prophet's children?
2. How would you feel if your pastor experienced marital difficulties like Hosea? How would you react if he explained it as a spiritual object lesson?
3. Do you think it would be easy to see Hosea as a true prophet? What types of statements do you think people could have made against him? What characteristics do Christians look for in those they consider as prophets?
4. Today, are people like Gomer given opportunity to mend their ways? Would Gomer be welcomed in most churches? Why or why not? What specific things can you do to help the "real" sinners within your world?
5. How does Paul use Hosea 1:10 and 2:23 in Romans 9:25, 26?

CHAPTER 2

Joel

The Prophet of Pentecost

One of the characteristics of the prophets is their frequent use of a current natural disaster to forecast the impending and inevitable judgement of God. They knew how to read the news and they saw God's hand in current events. One might say that the prophets were social commentators with eyes focused on earth but their ears attuned to heaven. The way Joel interprets his times is very interesting.

Unlike Amos, Micah, Zechariah and others who give us clues in their opening verses, the prophet Joel gives no insights about the date of his prophecy. No kings are mentioned. The land of Judah is referred to but not the land of Israel and the cruel invading army is unnamed. This lack of detail may indicate a kind of prophetic urgency in Joel. For what the people are about to face there is time only for repentance and faith.

From the very first chapter it is obvious that Joel, whose name means "Jehovah is God," is writing the Word of the Lord. An unprecedented plague of locusts had invaded and ravaged the land of Judah, and Joel has now challenged the elders, "Has anything like this ever happened in your days or in the days of your forefathers?" It was quite a disaster and the prophet expects the answer, "No, it's the worst we have ever seen." Joel is getting ready to draw spiritual lessons from this event. He approached this natural devastation in an attention-grabbing manner.

The plague of locusts was unbelievably destructive. It was an unimaginable horror: "What the locust swarm has left the great locusts have eaten; what the great locusts have left the young locusts have eaten; what the young locusts have left other locusts have eaten" (1:4). The people have no grapes to make wine! The farmers have no harvest to provide their livelihood. The priests have no grain or drink offerings for their temple worship. In an agricultural based society, it is hard to imagine anything more damaging.

In the face of such a mammoth pestilence we might expect the prophet of God to speak some encouraging words. We would, in terrible times, like to hear, "Cheer up! Things are bad but they are going to get better. Every cloud has a silver lining. Think positively!" After all, those in the ministry of the Lord are expected to offer hope. However, Joel does the precise opposite of this. Instead of suggesting that there is light at the end of the tunnel, he argues that the worst trouble is still to come! He seems to say, "You think this is bad? Just wait 'til later." The devestation of the locusts was horrible and total, but it will be nothing compared to the day of the Lord, the coming day of God's judgment: "What a dreadful day! For the day of the Lord is near; it will come like a destruction from the Almighty" (1:15).

There are two images of the locust invasion in this prophecy of Joel. In chapter one the picture is a very literal one. However, in chapter two the picture changes from a literal plague of insects to an image of an even greater army of invaders. Joel is warning the people of Judah that the original, literal invasion of locusts described in the first chapter has the prophetic significance of being a fore-shadowing of the inevitable and imminent day of the Lord: "Let all who live in the land tremble, for the day of the Lord is coming. It is close at hand" (2:1). The prophet is sounding a warning so that the people may prepare themselves for the storm that is threatening on the horizon.

THE DAY OF THE LORD

The day of the Lord is a major theme in the Minor Prophets. It is a technical phrase used to designate the future period of catastrophic judgment which will come upon the earth. The Hebrew mind divided time into two basic divisions: the present age, which is characterized by evil, and the age to come, the future kingdom of God, which will be characterized by righteousness. The day of the Lord marked the dividing point between the ages, with the coming of Messiah actually effecting the transition with a triumphant victory over the forces of evil.

As we know from the study of Bible prophecy, the prophets did not see as clearly as the New Testament writers but much more clearly than we often think (cf. 1 Peter 1:10-12). The prophets were unable to make an explicit distinction between the first and the second comings of Messiah. They saw time in two great divisions, the present evil age and the age to come, or the kingdom of God, which would begin when Messiah came. The New Testament shows that Christ began his spiritual kingdom when he came the first time. Many Christians think that the literal millennial kingdom will begin after his second advent. What this means is that, in a sense, the kingdom is here already, and in another sense it is not yet here. Christians are living in the period of time sometimes referred to as "the already but not yet." That is, the first coming of Christ inaugurated the kingdom of God, but it remains for the second coming of Christ to consummate the kingdom. Just before that happens, the terrible day of the Lord will take place. It is that time when God will break into history to judge the nation of Israel and all other nations. It is the final disaster, the time of great tribulation which will precede the second coming of Christ.

THE PURPOSE OF THE PROPHECY: REPENTANCE

What is Joel's purpose in prophesying the coming judgment? Is he simply a pessimist and a complainer? Is he a person who sees the glass as half-empty rather than half-full? No! The obvious reason for his dark comments is to lead the people to repentance. God wants his people prepared.

> The Lord thunders at the head of his army; his forces are beyond number, and mighty are those who obey his command. The day of the Lord is great; it is dreadful. Who can endure it? "Even now," declares the Lord, "return to me with all your heart, with fasting and weeping and mourning" (2: 11-12).

When the prophet begins to speak about repentance, he lays emphasis upon the heart. Repentance is a change of heart. In biblical psychology, the heart is the seat of the emotions and the core governing centre of human personality. Shallow religious rituals and mere outward forms of piety never impress God. God is not interested in the advertising we promote about ourselves; he is interested in the quality of the product we produce. God sees past the outward appearance and focuses on the condition of the heart. "Rend your hearts and not your garments," pleads the prophet (2: 13). It is easier to do the opposite. God demands not penance but penitence—genuine repentance. Parading of pharisaical piety may impress some people, but not God, and it will not save us in the day of wrath.

Spiritual integrity is not negotiable in our walk with God. Therefore, when we repent we have to go beyond the mere appearance of godly sorrow. We ought to note three things that characterize true repentance. Firstly, true repentance must involve a genuine confession of moral guilt before God, whom we have offended by our sin. This confession presupposes an agreement entered into which stipulated certain rules. In the covenant, God's people had a covenantal relationship with him that they had broken. Acknowledgement of that is the first step in restoration or reconciliation. Secondly, this confession must spring from a heart that is contrite and broken. There is no room for putting on a brave face. There is no room for pretending things aren't so bad or that we are not really to blame. There is no use pointing the finger at others. Only a tearing of our own hearts before God will free us from sin and enable us to escape the ultimate judgment. Thirdly, our confession must be attested by a life that is converted to the ways of God. It means a complete "about face" or, as C. S. Lewis once said, "Full speed astern." We cannot stop at the recognition of our sin, nor can we be satisfied with a sense of regret that we are sinners. We must, by the enabling grace of God, turn around and head away from our sin and pursue the path of righteousness.

The prophet calls for a solemn assembly, which was a period of holy fasting and a season of calling unto the Lord (1:14-15). You will notice that the call to repentance goes out to everyone old and young alike. No one is exempted from this call.

> Blow the trumpet in Zion, declare a holy fast, call a sacred assembly. Gather the people, consecrate the assembly; bring together the elders, gather the children, those nursing at the breast. Let the bridegroom leave his room and the bride her chamber. Let the priests, who minister before the Lord, weep between the porch and the altar. Let them say, "Spare your people, O Lord" (2:15-17).

INCENTIVE FOR REPENTANCE: THE GRACE OF GOD

Joel urges his people, "Return to the Lord your God, for he is gracious and compassionate, slow to anger and abounding in love" (2:13). Despite the dramatic and graphic beginning of his prophecy, the grace of God, not the fear of punishment, is the prophet's proclaimed motive for repentance. The call to repent is always linked to the promise of mercy. Martin Luther, the great Protestant reformer, wrote:

> To teach that repentance is to be reached by merely meditating upon sin and its consequences, is lying, stinking, seducing hypocrisy. We ought, first of all, to look into the wounds of Christ, and see in them His love toward us and our ingratitude towards Him, and thus with heartfelt affection to Christ and detestation of self, to meditate upon our sins. That is a true contrition and a fruitful repentance (LW III:47).

BENEFITS OF REPENTANCE: THE PROMISE OF THE SPIRIT

> Be not afraid, O land; be glad and rejoice. Surely the Lord has done great things. Be not afraid, O wild animals, for the open pastures are becoming green. The trees are bearing their fruit; the fig tree and the vine yield their riches. Be glad O people of Zion, rejoice in the Lord your God, for he has given you a teacher of righteousness. He sends you abundant showers, both autumn and spring rains, as before. The threshing floors will be filled with grain; that vats will overflow with new wine and oil. I will repay you for the years the locusts have eaten (2:21-25).

If we repent, God will restore the years that the locusts have eaten (2:21-27). What a promise! "And afterward, I will pour out my Spirit on all people" (2:28). The blessings which follow true repentance are often material, but there are always spiritual benefits first. The full repayment of lost fortunes will be in the millennial kingdom after the day of the Lord. Until that time some Christians enjoy some measure of material blessings, but not all and not always. Rain falls on the just and the unjust, and those believers living in-between the times still have to contend with sin, the world and the devil. Apart from the return of Christ our bodies will eventually fail and die. We have some blessings now already, yet the complete package awaits the final establishment of Christ's kingdom. It is a wise Christian who is patient and does not selfishly demand here and now what God has reserved for then and there.

According to Peter, in Acts 2:17-21, the events on the day of Pentecost were a fulfillment of Joel's prophecy. The "last days" began to run their course in the early days of the church and will end when Christ comes again in glory. We are now living in the climatic period of human history. Acts 2:39 reads, "The promise is for you and your children and for all who are afar off—for all whom the Lord our God will call." Joel's prophecy continues to be fulfilled as God's people come into the wonderful experience of the promise.

"Upon all flesh" indicates that the promise of the Spirit is worldwide in significance. No one group can monopolize the Holy Spirit. No Christian fellowship can afford to be sectarian and self-centered. In between the times the church must be a channel of blessing to all peoples in all places.

As disaster after disaster troubles our world, we must, like Joel, see in them the foreboding of the end of the age. We must not despair but have hope. We should realize that the door of grace is still open, although many think it is about to close, and we must turn in repentance to our gracious God, who still waits to forgive. Those who have repented and have experienced the promise of the Father must be ambassadors and witnesses, continuing the prophetic call to a world that is still in "the valley of decision."

The image of a valley of decision is a powerful one. To be caught in indecision is dangerous because God's judgment will soon be poured out. The gospel carries stern warnings as well as promises. The harvest is ripe for the outpouring of both judgment and grace. How good God is to order events so that an offer of grace precedes judgment! "God is not willing that any should perish, but that all should come to repentance" (2 Peter 3:9 KJV).

Joel ends his prophecy with a promise from God. The Lord says, "I will pardon" (3:21). If we turn in true repentance to God and trust in Christ alone for salvation, then our sins have been dealt with at Calvary and we will stand without condemnation when the last day dawns upon the earth.

QUESTIONS FOR REFLECTION

1. The tearing of the garments in Joel 2:13 was an outward display of repentance. How should genuine repentance be demonstrated?
2. How do you think Joel would interpret the horrible events that are often in our newscasts today?
3. How does Peter use Joel's prophecy to explain the events in Acts 2? Would Acts 2:38-39 suggest that Joel's prophecy continues to be fulfilled today?
4. Why did Joel counsel the blowing of a trumpet in Zion? (2:1, 15)
5. How is the day of the Lord described in Joel?
6. What promises in Joel have special meaning for you?

CHAPTER 3

Amos

The Farmer from Tekoa

Amos was a man without credentials, a man with no professional pedigree. No diplomas were hanging on his office walls. No degrees came after his name. No biography was written about his life or documentary made about his ministry. He knew none of the right people. Nor was he a man of experience. He was not a prophet, so he claimed, and he had not grown up in a prophet's home. In the eyes of the world there was no one quite so insignificant as this farmer from Tekoa. Yet he had a word from the Lord.

Amos ministered in a social context of affluence and exploitation. In an age not unlike our own if we look past the technology and focus on human behavior. The major interests of the people were profit-making and sensual indulgence. The leaders of the nation were irresponsible and unresponsive to the situation. Religion had been reduced to the ritualistic and public morality was at low tide.

It was a tough time to be a preacher but it was also a time that required a tough preacher.

SINS AGAINST CONSCIENCE (1:3-2:3)

> The words of Amos, one of the shepherds of Tekoa—what he saw concerning Israel two years before the earthquake, when Uzziah was king of Judah and Jeroboam son of Jehoash was king of Israel. He said: "The Lord roars from Zion and thunders from Jerusalem; the pastures of the shepherds dry up, and the top of Carmel withers." This is what the Lord says: "For three sins of Damascus, even for four, I will not turn back my wrath" (1:1-3).

Amos arrived on the scene rather suddenly. He pronounced the judgment of God upon the surrounding peoples of Damascus, Gaza, Tyre, Edom, Ammon and Moab. These peoples had been guilty of sinning against conscience, of inhuman cruelty, slave trading, racism and absolute disrespect for human life (1:3-2:3). The list was long.

One can easily imagine that the people of Israel, whom Amos was addressing, were favorably impressed. After all, the people of those neighboring cities were the enemies of God's people and outside the covenant bond. They were, indeed, without the special privileges of Israel. They were also guilty of all the atrocities of which they had been accused. Everyone knew that. It wasn't news to them and it might have seemed the prophet was heard gladly at first because he was reinforcing their prejudices. He was undoubtedly applauded as he denounced one city after another.

The applauding stopped very quickly though, and an uncomfortable silence reigned when Amos said, "For three transgressions of JUDAH, and for four, I will not revoke the punishment. . . . For three transgressions of ISRAEL, and for four, I will not revoke the punishment" (2:4,6 RSV). As the focus shifted from the enemies of God's people to God's people themselves, things changed. No longer was the prophet a champion of his people. It's amazing how much criticism we will tolerate about our enemies and how little we will tolerate about ourselves! Here Amos now points his condemning finger straight at Judah and Israel.

SINS AGAINST REVELATION (2:4-3:16)

Judah and Israel were condemned because they had sinned against revelation. They had the special privilege of having the law of God. It was a gift of God to them. They had a magnificent temple and the priesthood. They had the voice of the prophets. They were special people with special revelation, but they had despised God's truth. They had become covetous, proud, immoral and indifferent to the oppression of the poor and needy. In order to compensate for their guilty consciences, they had set up sacred shrines at Gilgal and Bethel. The only proper place to worship was at the temple in Jerusalem, which the people of the northern kingdom of Israel apparently neglected. They devoted themselves to solemn assemblies, sacrifices and offerings. They had the special events their religion specified. However, it seemed to be limited to the sanctuary. Outside the four walls they were no better for it. God was not impressed in the least. He said, "I hate, I despise your feasts, and I take no delight in your solemn assemblies. . . . But let justice roll down like waters, and righteousness like an everflowing stream" (5:21-24 RSV). One can't escape the emphasis on social justice in Amos. The worship of God cannot be limited to inward personal piety and outward religious rituals. True worship makes itself evident in our just and righteous relationships. It is seen in how we treat people.

THE ROAR OF THE LION UNHEEDED

Amos pictured God as a lion about ready to spring upon its prey. "The lion has roared—who will not fear? The Sovereign Lord has spoken—who can but prophesy? (3:8). It was a fear inspiring message. Unfortunately, his ministry was not well received. Guess who resisted it the most! Yes, the religious leadership of the times. The ecclesiastical authority, in the person of Amaziah the priest of Bethel, wanted to get rid of the prophet (7:10-13). He did not wish to hear about empty ritualism, social injustice, immorality, materialism and rebellion against the covenant. In fact, sin was openly committed right in the place of worship (2:7-8). No sin is so abhorrent to God, so injurious to his work, or so hard to root out as that which is committed under the cloak of religion. But, a reckoning day is coming.

What is surprising about the sin of Israel and Judah was their misunderstanding of the day of the Lord. Sin does strange things to people. If we know what is right but fail to do it, soon we forget what is right. Persistent sin will entrap us and deceive us into thinking that our wrong action is actually right! Sin distorts our sense of moral values and dulls our moral discernment. This is what happened to Israel. They assumed the day of judgment was still in the distant future (6:3). They believed there was plenty of time to live it up. Actually, by their deeds they were hastening the judgment day!

The people of Judah and Israel were looking forward to the day of the Lord with anticipation as if God were pleased with their behavior! But for them, the day of the Lord would not be a day of blessing. It would be a day of judgment:

> Woe to you who long for the day of the Lord! Why do you long for the day of the Lord? That day will be darkness, not light. It will be as though a man fled from a lion only to meet a bear, as though he entered his house and rested his hand

on the wall only to have a snake bite him. Will not the day of the Lord be darkness, not light—pitch-dark, without a ray of brightness? (5:18-20).

"HEAR THIS WORD"

Chapters three to five begin with "Hear this word." Amos is especially perturbed by the affluent lifestyle of the women of Samaria, whom he sarcastically calls "cows of Bashan," interested only in lazy, luxurious living (4:1). It was not the most politically correct statement to make, but the men were no better. Oblivious to the danger, they apparently spent their time lying around on ivory beds and other opulent furniture (6:3-4). They used the most expensive aftershaves, ate at the finest restaurants, guzzled the finest of wines by the gallon to the noise of worldly music (6:4-6). They were completely unaffected by the hurt and desperate needs of their fellowman. "You do not grieve over the ruin of Joseph" (6: 6). Does this sound familiar?

Amos was not pleased with this. In the eyes of the prophet the people were sinning. Such sumptuous living was not a sign of blessing. It was not evidence that all was right between them and God. Amos was not a theologian of prosperity. For him such wealth and hedonistic comfort was vanity. One shudders to think that Amos would say to those evangelicals today who preach that wealth is a sign of spiritual health. Although one could surmise that many might reject him as an uncultured backwoods preacher unaccustomed to big city life!

The prophetic visions of a locust swarm, a fire, a plumb line, a basket of fruit and the Lord standing at the altar ready to judge serve as warnings. When measured against God's standards, Israel was found wanting. Even though the judgment upon Israel would be harsh, the nation would not totally be destroyed. A remnant would be saved, and God would restore the Davidic kingdom in the last days (3:12, 9:11-15).

> "In that day I will restore David's fallen tent. I will repair its broken places, restore its ruins, and build it as it used to be, so that they may possess the remnant of Edom and all the nations that bear my name," declares the Lord, who will do these things. "The days are coming," declares the Lord, "when the reaper will be overtaken by the plowman and the planter by the one treading grapes. New wine will drip from the mountains and flow from all the hills I will bring back my exiled people Israel; they will rebuild the ruined cities and live in them. They will plant vineyards and drink their wine; they will make gardens and eat their fruit. I will plant Israel in their own land, never again to be uprooted from the land I have given them," says the Lord your God (9:11-15).

LESSONS FROM AMOS

Several lessons are to be learned from the prophet's message. The first and most obvious is that special privilege carries special responsibility. It is dangerous to be "at ease in Zion." If we allow ourselves to be "at ease," we will become insensitive to the needs around us. We will become mere spectators of the Lord's work rather than participators in it. Also, to be "at ease in Zion" causes us to be unaware of our spiritual danger. Israel and Judah thought that privilege brought security. They were wrong! The closer we are to God, the closer we are to his scrutiny and judgment. To whom much is given, much is required.

A second lesson is that past blessings are no security from God's judgments. Our moral commitment and spiritual experience must be up-to-date. God had, indeed, brought Israel out of Egypt. He had chosen her from all the families in the world. Israel had a glorious past. She was special to God. But now she had not heeded the warnings sent from God. She had not returned to God (4: 6, 8, 10,11). She had built substitute sanctuaries, false places of worship. The prophet pleads, "Prepare to meet your God, O Israel" (4:12).

A third lesson to learn is that ritual without reality is repulsive to God. The mere profession of religion is inadequate. A "going through the motions" is meaningless. Our religious profession must be verified by a true response to God's grace. We should exhibit a willingness to hear and receive the word of the Lord. Our lives should be characterized by humble obedience to God and an unselfish love for the oppressed and the needy.

A fourth lesson to be learned concerns wealth and affluence. The focus of Israel's love was her selfish gain, not her sovereign Lord. Our materialistic age poses great threats to sinner and saint alike. How easy it is to become covetous. The envy of other people's successes can be the root of much injustice. We think, "It isn't fair." This leads to gossip and personality assassination for example. How easy it is to neglect the financial support of the Lord's work. How easy it is to feather one's own nest. The "blessings" of our day can become a "curse" upon our heads. If our riches increase, let us neither set our hearts upon them nor build a "theology" to justify our good fortune.

A final lesson we may learn from Amos is the danger of judging people on the basis of their social or economical status. Most likely Amos was rejected because of this. He was not an "upper-class" man. We must learn not to reject God's word merely because the messenger is not of our liking. God does not always use educated individuals like Paul or eloquent persons like Apollos. He often uses the simple things of the world to confound the mighty. In our best moments we know that to be true. Good coffee can be served in a plain mug or in a fine china cup with saucer! Does it matter that much? Amos may not have had all the right qualifications, but he knew God, and that's all that really matters. His message is still valid: "This is what the Lord says to the house of Israel: Seek me and live; do not seek Bethel, do not go to Gilgal, do not journey to Beersheba. . . . Seek the Lord and live" (5:4-6).

QUESTIONS FOR REFLECTION

1. What verses in Amos give evidence that God's prophets could use sarcasm in their messages? How would you react if your faults were highlighted in that manner?
2. How does God speak today? Does he use only the still small voice? Note Amos 3:8. How does God speak like a roaring lion today?
3. How many times in chapter 4 does God lament that his people have not returned to him? How would we know if people turned to God today? What evidence should we expect to see in the private and public life of people who heed God's call to return?
4. How do you think Amos would respond to this question? "Should preachers be involved in politics?"
5. Are the sins in the days of Amos similar to the sins of our day?
6. What verses in Amos were especially convicting for you? What verses were especially comforting? Why?

CHAPTER 4

Obadiah

The Prophet of Doom

The "Minor" Prophets get that title because of the relative shortness of their messages compared to the length of such "Major" Prophets as Isaiah, Ezekiel and Jeremiah. There are a total of 67 chapters in all the Minor Prophets together compared to 66 chapters in Isaiah alone. The "Minor" Prophets, however, are in no way inferior to the "Major" Prophets. Bigger is not necessarily better. The little book of Obadiah is a case in point. We all know the old saying, "Never judge a book by its cover." In the case of Obadiah we can easily say, "Never judge a book by its length."

Little if anything is known about the life and circumstances of this prophet. About a dozen people in the Old Testament bear the name Obadiah, which means "servant or worshipper of Jehovah." His personality was not particularly pertinent to his prophecy – the message is always more important than the messenger, and Obadiah had a vision from the Lord that was focused on one particular nation.

The prophet Obadiah was presumably from Judah, to the south of which was the land of Edom. Edom was a very prosperous country and was naturally fortified by high mountains and cliffs of red rocks. Prosperity and military security were the trademarks of the Edomites. Such advantages were the root causes of their national arrogance. It was because of this unwarranted pride and the resultant cruelty expressed against the people of God during the fall of Jerusalem (587 B.C.) that God caused Obadiah the prophet to speak a message of doom.

THE WARNINGS AGAINST EDOM (1-9)

> This is what the sovereign Lord says about Edom – We have heard a message from the Lord: An envoy was sent to the nations to say, "Rise, and let us go against her for battle" —"See, I will make you small among the nations; you will be utterly despised. The pride of your heart has deceived you, you who live in the clefts of the rocks and make your home on the heights, you who say to yourself, 'Who can bring me down to the ground?' Though you soar like the eagle and make your nest among the stars, from there I will bring you down," declares the Lord (vv. 1-4).

The prophet wasted no time in declaring that Edom's problem was one of national pride, an over-inflated national self-consciousness. They felt themselves secure in their mountain fortresses. They felt themselves as safe as an eagle in its nest. The eagle in North America is a symbol of freedom; it has no natural enemies. Edom felt they were free from limits and restraints, but they were not free from God's judgment. "Who will bring me down to the ground?" they boasted, as if their destruction were impossible. But the Lord said, "I will bring you down." Edom's attitude was the height of pride and self-deception. Such an attitude always goes before destruction (Proverbs 16:18).

The prophet warned that the devastation of Edom would be so great that nothing would remain. Sometimes thieves, after taking what they want, will leave a few things. Even grape pickers leave some grapes on the vines! However, Edom's humiliation can only be described as absolute.

EDOM'S SINS AND JUDGMENT (10-16)

> You should not look down on your brother in the day of his misfortune, nor rejoice over the people of Judah in the day of their destruction, nor boast so much in the day of their trouble (v. 12).

Edom's sins were particularly horrid because they were sins against their own relatives. The Edomites were descended from Esau, whose brother Jacob was the ancestor of the Israelites. The history of the relationship between the two peoples is a long and sad story of hatred and animosity. Enmity had existed between the brothers from childhood. Esau's offspring continued the struggle throughout history. When the children of Israel wanted to cross the territory of Edom on their way to the promised land, the Edomite king refused to let them through (Numbers 20:14-21). The first three kings of Israel, Saul, David and Solomon, had constant problems with their relatives to the south (1 Samuel 14: 47; 1 Kings 11:14-25). According to Psalm 137:7, the Edomites rejoiced at Nebuchadnezzar's victory over Jerusalem. Family hatred is sometimes the hardest to resolve.

The prophet Obadiah made a list of the sins committed by Edom against his brother Jacob. Some of the sins were passive, reminiscent of those who passed by the man who fell among thieves in the parable of the Good Samaritan. One, they stood aloof when foreigners invaded and carried off Israel's wealth (v. 11). Two, the Edomites even gloated and rejoiced over the misfortune of their brother (v. 12). But Edom was also guilty of sins of an active nature. The Edomites actually entered into the city, looting and preventing the escape of refugees, even betraying them to the enemy (vv. 13-14). Such sins could not go unnoticed by God, neither would they go unpunished.

The bottom line in the whole prophecy is, of course, verse 15; "For the day of the Lord is near upon all nations. As you have done, it shall be done to you, your deeds shall return on your own head" (RSV). It is a principle common throughout the Bible. Nations and individuals reap what they sow unless they come to the Lord for mercy. According to Obadiah, Edom was on a one-way trip to doom and disaster. Judgment will be meted out to all the wicked. The tables will be turned in the day of God's judgment.

Obadiah's voice rang with poetic justice. The Edomites who drank wine in celebrating the fall of Jerusalem will then drink the wine of God's wrath and "shall be as though they had not been" (v. 16 RSV). There are powerful and dramatic words. Today the prophecy is fulfilled, for Edom is a wilderness and wasteland.

THE RESTORATION OF ISRAEL (17-21)

> But on Mount Zion will be deliverance; it will be holy, and the house of Jacob will possess its inheritance (v. 17).

The silver lining in the cloud of Edom's destruction is Israel's deliverance. There will come a reversal of Israel's misfortunes. As the prophet Joel said, God "will restore to you the years that the locust hath eaten" (Joel 2:25 KJV). The last part of Obadiah's prophecy is the assurance that God will triumph and Israel will be restored. Israel will possess her possessions and divinely appointed rulers will lead her. The kingdom shall be the Lord's! What encouragement this is for all God's people in every age.

LEARNING FROM EDOM'S SINS

The sins of Edom serve as warnings to us, and we must learn from them. First, we must learn that a false sense of security can bring devastating consequences. For the Christian, the Lord is our refuge and strength, not the mountains of Edom. We must trust neither in our national security nor in our own understanding; we must depend on the arm of God! Patriotism is no substitute for a relationship with the Lord.

Secondly, we must be aware of the danger of pride. National pride is nothing more than the sum total of individual pride. God hates pride in any form. In our day great emphasis is placed on self-esteem. We have innumerable books on loving yourself. Someone has called our times "the age of narcissism." Many Christian writers, in an effort to help depressed believers, twist the second part of the great commandment to love your neighbor as yourself to mean "love yourself." There may be a fine line between a healthy self-concept and the love of self that is the greatest idolatry. Humility is still a Christian virtue, and it is the opposite of pride. Let's not hide sinful pride under a cloak of self-esteem. The refrain of an old song says it well:

> Humble thyself and the Lord will draw near thee.
> Humble thyself and his presence will cheer thee.
> He will not walk with the proud or the scornful.
> Humble thyself to walk with God.

Thirdly, we should give God the glory for any prosperity or advantages we enjoy. All good gifts come from our heavenly father and we should remember that. Edom did not. Many Old Testament scholars believe pride was the original sin of Satan (Isaiah 14:13-14). Apparently Edom was proud, not only of her natural advantages, but also of her wisdom and understanding (v.8). God can do more with an idiot and a fool than he can with a man puffed up with conceit. As John Calvin once said, "If we excel in understanding, we are not to abuse this singular gift of God." The gifts that God gives are to be used in faithful service to others and thereby give honor back to God.

Fourthly, we must guard against hatred because it always produces evil and sinful behavior. If we are guilty of the passive sin of looking down on others or taking secret pleasure in their misfortune, it won't be long before we, ourselves, will be sinning in a more active manner. Sinful attitudes are the seeds of sinful actions. Unless they are changed they will grow up to choke our spiritual life.

Fifthly, we should be assured that our God is the Lord of human history and that he will eventually punish the nations for their crimes against his people Israel. The prophet Obadiah is the only prophet to speak solely against a foreign nation, yet verse 15 indicates that the day of the Lord is near for all nations. Anti-Semitism is a dangerous policy. Not everything the nation of Israel does is right, and God will take special measures to deal with his own people. We dare not presume to do God's work of judgment. The great promise God made to Israel still remains in Scripture: "I will bless them that bless thee, and will curse them that curse thee" (Genesis 12:3 KJV). God is aware of the cruelty done to his people. Let all nations take heed.

This assurance of God's ultimate control over human affairs should help us to take heart in the face of affliction. It must have been difficult for Israel to be living in a period of devastation while their enemies were celebrating their misfortune. The prosperity of the wicked and the suffering of the righteous are great mysteries that will be unraveled and eternally reversed when the day of the Lord comes. Our God is a God of justice and he calls us to live justly. He will judge nations and individuals for their sins, but he will also correct the wrong done to his people, if not in this life, most assuredly in the life to come. The righteous often find it difficult to wait patiently for God's justice, and there is much we can do to reverse the social injustice that we see around us. We need wisdom to know if the injustice is within our purview. Revenge most certainly is not. We must do all we can. Yet, when faced with unjust situations beyond our control we can still face life optimistically because we know God is still in control.

We have called Obadiah the prophet of doom. Indeed, he does have a message of doom for all those who do not follow the Lord. God will send judgment upon the enemies of his people. But his great hand of deliverance will be outstretched towards those who trust in his name.

> Deliverers will go up on Mount Zion to govern the mountains of Esau. And the kingdom will be the Lord's (v. 21).

QUESTIONS FOR REFLECTION

1. Why does God hate pride? What other Old Testament texts warn against this sin?
2. List the specific sins in verses 10-14. Are there any similar sins being committed today?
3. How would Obadiah respond to those who say sin is a matter of action, not attitude?
4. Do you think Obadiah would be for or against the arms race? What would he say to the major military powers today?
5. We have called Obadiah the prophet of doom. What evidence is there of optimism in his prophecy?

CHAPTER 5

JONAH

The Disobedient Prophet

Jonah is the best known of the twelve Minor Prophets and his story is a favorite of the many Sunday school children who sing "I don't want to be a Jonah and be swallowed by a whale." However, the fact of its familiarity is probably the reason why it is possible to miss the very essence of the message. We short-change ourselves if we get sidetracked into measuring the size of the fish's mouth or risk stepping into the quicksand of whether or not there is myth in the Bible. The significance of the story doesn't emerge from such discussions as important as many consider them to be.

The prophet Jonah received a divine directive to preach to the wicked city of Nineveh (1:1-2), but he immediately evaded his responsibility by taking a ship to the distant city of Tarshish (1: 3). He heard from God and he ran! Who wouldn't? After all, in Scripture, the Almighty doesn't present himself as a big cuddly stuffed toy or a genie in a bottle. The prophet Isaiah was awestruck when he realized the divine presence in the temple. He didn't run but he wasn't comfortable either. Isaiah asked to be sent from his presence to accomplish his mission. Jonah wanted to escape from his presence to avoid his mission. While en route God sent a great storm which threatened the ship and the lives of all on board (1: 4-10). The experienced sailors were unusually troubled by the sudden storm and sought to placate their pagan gods. Eventually Jonah was discovered to be responsible for the disaster. In response to their inquiry, Jonah persuaded the mariners to throw him into the raging sea, whereupon the storm ceased (1: 11-16).

God, the main actor in the whole series of events, ordained a huge sea creature to swallow the prophet, who remained in his subterranean prison for three days and three nights (1:17). From this distressful place Jonah desperately prayed to God in repentance and thanksgiving:

> "When my life was ebbing away, I remembered you, Lord, and my prayer rose to you, to your holy temple. Those who cling to worthless idols forfeit the grace that could be theirs. But I, with a song of thanksgiving, will sacrifice to you. What I have vowed I will make good. Salvation comes from the Lord" (2: 7-9).

In response to this urgent prayer, the Lord delivered him in a unique manner (2:1-10).

> Then the word of the Lord came to Jonah a second time: "Go to the great city of Nineveh and proclaim to it the message I give you." Jonah obeyed the word of the Lord and went to Nineveh . . . He proclaimed: "Forty more days and Nineveh will be destroyed." The Ninevites believed God. They declared a fast, and all of them, from the greatest to the least, put on sackcloth (3:1-5).

Jonah received a second chance and was re-commissioned by God (3:1-2). His immediate obedience and subsequent preaching of impending judgment (3:3-4) brought about the repentance of both king and people which resulted in divine forgiveness (3:5-10): "When God saw what they did and how they turned from their evil ways, he had compassion and did not bring upon them the destruction he had threatened" (3:10).

Jonah was chagrined (4:1). He was so severely depressed and angry over God's willingness to forego judgment and extend mercy that he wanted to die (4:2-3). In desperation he sat down under a self-made shelter and the Lord created a plant to give him shade until a worm caused it to wither. The hot eastern sun was so scorching that, in anger, Jonah wished for death. The Lord chided him for his unreasonable reaction because the prophet's attitude stood in such sharp contrast to the compassion of the Almighty for Nineveh (4:4-11).

The story of Jonah is exciting and fast-moving. In comparison with the other prophetic books, it is free of long prophetic speeches. There are no long lists of curses and blessings. There is very little detail of the wickedness of the people. Except for the short statement in 3:4, "Yet forty days and Nineveh will be overthrown," there are no prophetic oracles to teach us. Nevertheless, we may still hear the word of God because the important truths in the book come to us by way of the narrative.

JONAH'S THEOLOGY

The major theological message of the book is that God wills to extend his saving grace beyond the borders of national Israel. God is not some angry monster who delights in the destruction of the wicked. He delights in saving sinners. The story of Jonah is an Old Testament illustration of John 3:16. God loves the whole world. The sovereign choice of Israel was not because God played "favorites." God is concerned about all people on earth. We need to see the world as God sees it. We need to love the world as God does!

The doctrine of God is particularly important for the Christian. Nothing is more dangerous to spiritual life as wrong thinking about God, so the study of the theology is not an option for the Christian. If one despises theology, he is saying it doesn't matter how one thinks about God. Reflection on the Holy Scriptures will give us a biblical theology, an understanding about God that is in accord with God's revelation in his Word. One of the major heretics in early church history was Marcion, who said the God of the Old Testament was not the true God but a vengeful, evil deity who took pleasure in killing people. He was wrong, and the church rejected his teaching because of its theological weaknesses.

Jonah's problem was not that he had a bad theology. His head was right, but his heart was wrong. It's so easy to have a discrepancy between belief and practice. He knew God was a gracious God, but he passionately disliked the idea of Nineveh having a chance to repent. The Bible says,

> But it greatly displeased Jonah, and he became angry. And he prayed to the Lord and said, "Please Lord, was not this what I said when I was still in my own country? Therefore, in order to forestall this I fled to Tarshish, for I knew that Thou art a gracious and compassionate God, slow to anger and abundant in loving-kindness, and one who relents concerning calamity" (4:1-2 NASB).

Jonah's problem was that he did not want anyone to be saved but his own people. Like the false teachers in Galatia to whom Paul wrote in the New Testament, the prophet wanted to limit grace to race. He was guilty of prejudice, jealousy and religious bigotry—not the best characteristics for a prophet! How frail we are!

LESSONS FROM JONAH

The book of Jonah illustrates that the possession of divine truth and privilege brings great responsibility. To whom much is given, much is required. Israel had a particular place in the heart of God, not because God had no love for anyone else, but because he had a special purpose for them. God saves us to serve. Missions is at the heart of God's plan for the church. "The Lord . . . is not willing that any should perish, but that all should come to repentance" (2 Peter 3:9 KJV). A Christian without a missionary heart is a contradiction in terms.

It is comforting to know that Jonah's disobedience did not frustrate the ultimate purposes of God. God will go to great lengths to get his will done. God was willing to smash anything which interfered with his sovereign plan. I'm sure the captain of that ship would advise anyone to think twice about aiding a prophet in his backsliding! The context is rather negative here, but it is possible for us to feel a sense of confidence in knowing that God is at work helping us to do his will. Of course, Jonah was to blame for his own troubles. Yet we may be encouraged to know that God is "for" us and, if our heart is right, he will bring down those things that keep us from being in the centre of his will.

However, one must not presume that God's grace will be endless or that we can disobey the Lord without serious consequence. God is most assuredly patient with his erring children, but there is a line which can be crossed. If we persistently fail to obey God, he will pass us by and use another as his channel of blessing.

The Jonah story teaches that the salvation of people costs! It requires a letting go of deeply ingrained attitudes. We must not allow the sins of racial or social prejudice to dominate our lives. Such sins will hinder our effectiveness as witnesses of the gospel. Jonah paid a price for his reluctance. He was thrown into the sea. Was his willingness to sacrifice his life the ultimate attempt to escape his responsibility, or was he genuinely concerned about the sailors? We can't be absolutely sure. Eventually God used him, but even then Jonah wasn't completely problem-free.

How easy it is to doubt the spiritual experiences of others who are not of our particular persuasion or social circle. The disciples of Jesus had a similar problem believing that uncircumcised Gentiles could be part of the church (cf. Mark 9:38-39; Luke 9:49-50; John 10:16; Acts chapters 10, 11, 15). We should be grateful to God for how far some people have come. Let's not reject them because they still have some distance to go.

We must not be jealous over the extension of mercy and grace to the apparently unworthy. We are all unworthy. That's what makes mercy, mercy! If we deserve it, it wouldn't be grace. Do we pray for an outpouring of the Spirit upon all flesh but fail to rejoice in what God is doing in other churches? Do we pray for our young people to be saved and yet verbally harass them about their dress or their music? Do we pray for our churches to grow but shun the unemployed, the drunkard and the divorced? Do we want God to save only certain kinds of sinners, or all kinds of sinners?

I have often wondered why the story of Jonah was in the Bible. It ends on a negative note and the character of the prophet revealed it isn't flattering. Aren't prophets all great men of God who can call down fire from heaven? Aren't they the models for preachers? How is it possible for Jonah to be a prophet and a depressed suicidal bigot at the same time? Who leaked such a story? Who would give such a full disclosure of the truth? Most preachers would be tempted to tell the news of the great revival meetings they held in Nineveh. Most would publish the positive results and hide the negative. But, not Jonah! Jonah is very transparent and for a very specific reason. We will have to wait until later to read the rest of Jonah's diary, if he ever kept one. What we do know is that Jonah is probably telling this story many years after the event. He survived the ocean cruise and he also survived his depression. Because of that, he can let us know the dark parts of his journey. It helps us to know that even great people of God like Jonah are, in the end, just people like us.

The book of Jonah teaches us another dynamic truth. Sometimes in this life we get a second chance. If we fail God, it doesn't mean that we are forever relegated to the ash heap of life. God is in the redeeming business. He saves real sinners, not just pretend ones! Prophets aren't perfect, and at times even a prophet can disappoint us. However, our faith must not be in the prophet but in the prophet's God. We must not worship spiritual heroes. Of course, when our spiritual heroes fall, we must not deny them our prayers and forgiveness. Someone has said that the Christian army is the only one that shoots its wounded! We must, by Christian compassion, show this to be incorrect while at the same time maintaining a high view of Christian holiness and staying on guard lest we fall into similar temptation (Galatians 6:1; 1 Corinthians 10:12).

God calls us to proclaim his truth in word and witness. The Jonah story shows the extent to which God went to enable the prophet to fulfill his mission. In the process we learn much about God and his desire to save people. However, we cannot conclude God will save them without our involvement or that he will always do such dramatic things to encourage our obedience. So, as they sing in Sunday school,

> Down to Nineveh I will go
> if my Saviour tells me so.
> And I'll shout aloud
> "Ye must be born again."

QUESTIONS FOR REFECTION

1. Why was Jonah reluctant to go to Nineveh?
2. Why did not God simply choose someone else instead of giving the prophet a second chance?
3. Does God give people a second chance to accomplish his will? Is it possible to miss God's best for our lives? Is it possible to

return to God's best? How can we avoid missing the will of God?

4. How would you describe Jonah's attitude towards Nineveh after they repented?
5. How does the New Testament refer to Jonah? (cf. Matthew 12: 39-41; Luke 11:29-30).

CHAPTER 6

Micah

The Prophet to the City

The Minor Prophets have earned a reputation for being proclaimers of doom and gloom. It is popular to imagine the ministry of a prophet as primarily negative and harsh. We see ample evidence in the scriptures that God uses strong prophets to point out the failings of his people and then point to the way back. Faithfulness to the covenant was their prime concern and they pulled no punches in their condemnation of impiety and social injustice. When their warnings were ignored, the predicted judgment was often swift in coming. Although intimations of grace are in all the prophets considered so far, the general picture is quite depressing in Hosea, Joel, Amos, Obadiah and Jonah. Micah, however, is a prophet with a difference. He, too, preached judgment, but a new note of hope was heard in his message. Like Jonah, Micah was heeded and judgment was delayed for 100 years.

Little is known of Micah's personal history. He was a contemporary of Isaiah and Hosea and is best known as the prophet who foretold the place of Christ's birth (5:2). Matthew's gospel quotes this prophecy in reference to Jesus' birth in Bethlehem (Matthew 2: 6). Like Amos, Micah was a country boy, uncomfortable with the fast pace of urban living and rather distrustful of the city (cf. 1:5). He is simply called "Micah of Moresheth," which may mean that he came from the tiny village of Moresheth-Gath, twenty-five miles southwest of Jerusalem.

His ministry was relatively long. He prophesied during the reign of three kings, Jotham, Ahaz and Hezekiah (740-687 B.C.). Jotham was a good king, but he did not destroy all the high places where pagan worship was performed (2 Chronicles 27). Ahaz was useless as a spiritual example, openly advocating idolatry. During his reign the northern kingdom of Israel fell and was taken into captivity (2 Chronicles 28). Revival happened only in the reign of the godly king Hezekiah, after more than two decades of faithful labor by the prophet Micah. Preaching doesn't always bring immediate results. It may take years before the seed that is sown ripens into a harvest. We are misled if we think that revival is simply a matter of getting the right "prophet" to hold meetings.

God gave Micah special insight to see beneath the shallow veneer of his society. It is like J. I. Packer once said about much of modern religion, "It's a mile wide but only an inch thick!" The prophet detected underneath the thin religious façade a multitude of festering sores, and he could not be silent. Like an evangelist with a strong social conscience, he uttered three prophetic oracles, each beginning with "Hear" (1:2, 3:1, 6:1). "Hear all you peoples!" "Hear now O heads of Jacob." "Hear now what the Lord says." How important it is to hear what God has to say about the turbulent times we are in. Each prophetic message contained a condemnation of sin and a promise of future hope if trust was placed in the Lord.

THE FIRST PROPHETIC ORACLE (1:1-2:13)

His first message of judgment was directed to the cities of Samaria and Jerusalem. While sin infects every human heart no matter where it lives, it seems as if in cities sin is more concentrated and covertly celebrated. At least, one gets the impression that the prophets think this way. Spiritual first aid could not cure the disease for "her wound is incurable" Micah teaches (1:9). Only the surgery of divine justice could deal with the matter.

IDOLATRY CONDEMNED

What was the problem? According to the prophet, it was the tolerance of a false religion of idolatry that had reached not only into Samaria, but also into the holy city of Jerusalem itself. The prophet shouted, "What is Judah's high place? Is it not Jerusalem?" (1:5). Such idolatry, in the eyes of God, was spiritual adultery, and the prophet was incensed with holy concern.

Idol worship in its various forms is very subtle, and it often takes a prophet to make us see those things in our lives that stand between us and God. Of course, a prophet must identify with the people. They must place their money where their mouths are, so to speak. It isn't sufficient for the man or woman of God to pontificate from the pulpit how people should live. They, too, must bring their lives into parallel with their message.

Micah ordered the leaders to shave their heads (1:16) as a demonstration of heartfelt repentance. One tear will do more to move the merciful hand of God than a thousand pious-sounding prayers that come from the lips alone. Nothing hinders true repentance like the preaching of mushy grace that thinks of as sin as no big matter. It's no big deal so why can't God just get over it? Such thinking must be abandoned.

Idols are created in our minds when we adopt an inferior and distorted concept of God. The Lord is not just a one dimensional big cuddly teddy bear of love that is soft on sin. We invent an idol by magnifying the love of God at the expense of the holy justice of God. In Micah 2:6, 7 we get the impression that the popular preachers of Micah's day were saying that God would not judge his people because it would be against his nature. "God never gets angry," they argued.

> "Do not prophesy," their prophets say. "Do not prophesy about these things; disgrace will not overtake us." Should it be said, O house of Jacob: Is the Spirit of the Lord angry? Does he do such things?

They had modified their concept of God until it no longer allowed for the "justice" of God. Micah, like most of the prophets, was also a theologian with a passion for a proper understanding of God and his ways. Much of our own sin today finds its roots in wrong thinking about the holiness and justice of God. After all, a "teddy bear" God need neither to be feared nor obeyed. However, for the true people of God, the fear of the Lord is still the beginning of wisdom.

MATERIALISM CONDEMNED

Their inadequate knowledge of God allowed the rulers of Micah's day to oppress the poor and the needy. They spent their time planning iniquity, plotting evil, coveting fields and houses and seizing them, defrauding people of their homes, and denying children their inheritance (2:1-2, 8-9). It's hard to imagine worse qualities in leaders and such situations are breeding grounds for rebellion. But Micah does not advocate that as a solution.

Materialism is not just a sin of corrupt leaders. Even God's people can be drawn into the quest of riches, and failing that in the clutches of envy. Christians must learn to be content. How easy it is for us to justify "grabbing a piece of the pie." Our money-oriented culture of glitter and gold tempts us with the great sins of envy and greed. These are sins which sometimes parade around in pious garments. The lazy life of luxurious selfishness cannot be atoned for by costly religious rituals like building towers and amusement parks in the name of God while the evangelistic and social work of the local church suffers for lack of support. Micah would see such splendid excesses as sinful.

Material prosperity can be a blessing from God; he does not place a premium on poverty. However, in Micah's day the methods and motives for getting wealthy were both wrong. The rich were getting richer and the poor were getting poorer. Oppression, greed and corruption were characteristic of the judicial, legislative and religious systems. Governmental leaders were exploitive, judges could be bought, prophets and priests alike were in it for what they could get out of it. Preachers were for sale, telling the people what they wanted to hear, not what God wanted them to speak. The people wanted their preachers to be prophets of prosperity and ease, not truth. In sarcasm Micah says, "If a liar and deceiver comes and says, 'I will prophesy for you plenty of wine and beer,' he would be just the prophet for this people!" (2:11). Sarcasm is a powerful whip in the hands of a prophet.

THE SECOND PROPHETIC ORACLE (3:1-5:15)

In the second major message this minor prophet places the spotlight on the sins of rulers, judges, false prophets and priests.

> This is what the Lord says:
>
> "As for the prophets who lead my people astray, if one feeds them they will proclaim 'peace'; if he does not, they prepare to wage war against him" (3:5).
>
> "Her leaders judge for a bribe, her priests teach for a price, and her prophets tell fortunes for money" (3:11a).

To make matters worse, they covered their sins in a religious cloak. "Yet they lean upon the Lord and say, 'Is not the Lord among us? No disaster will come upon us'" (3:11b). There is no hypocrisy as distasteful as that of religious people who lack moral integrity. Quite often we applaud the prophets when they speak against our enemies. We are so skilled in perceiving sin in others. But we ought also to apply the prophet's message to ourselves. Sin goes to church in Sunday clothes as often as it goes anywhere. Judgment must begin at the house of the Lord. How can Christians condemn the sins of the world and sweep their own sins under the carpet? The Lord isn't pleased with that and those involved are living on borrowed time. Soon God will reduce them to rubble (3:12).

In the fourth and fifth chapters, the picture changes and Micah predicts a future time of peace and great prosperity for God's people, associated with the first and second comings of Messiah (4: 1-5:12). The destruction of the city of Jerusalem would not mean the total destruction of the people of God. The future would reveal a restoration in the last days (4:1). A remnant will survive and be blessed by God (4:7). Whole nations will come to Jerusalem and learn the ways of the Lord.

THE THIRD PROPHETIC ORACLE (6:1-7:20)

After having finished with his condemnation of Samaria and Judah, Micah's third message is a divine indictment against the nation of Israel and her sins. The prophet wasn't just an old "hippie" with a hatred for social bureaucracies and nostalgia for the simplicity of rustic life. He was aware that the actual situation in politics, economics and religion was displeasing to God.

There is a danger in sanctifying the status quo. God's spiritual leaders must not be silent in sinful situations, lest they support sin. In the time of Amos, Amaziah the priest supported the corrupt government. When religious leaders work hand in glove with governments that are unconcerned with the poor and the outcast, we are in dire circumstances indeed. Some religious leaders are vocal against private sins of individuals, and so they should be. However, we must all raise our voices in harmony with the prophet against the sin of poverty where and when the poor are victims of oppression and greed. We must also empty our full closets and cupboards to clothe the naked and feed the hungry. We cannot lay a claim to a good relationship with God while maintaining a bad relationship with the less fortunate.

Despite the many blessings received from God, his people had turned their backs on him and their religion was a failure "where the rubber meets the road." They had forsaken justice; they had failed to show mercy and they had refused to walk in humility before God.

> With what shall I come before the Lord and bow down before the exalted God? Shall I come before him with burnt offerings, with calves a year old? Will the Lord be pleased with thousands of rams, with ten thousand rivers of oil? Shall I offer my firstborn for my transgressions, the fruit of my body for the sin of my soul? He has showed you, O man, what is good. And what does the Lord require of you? To act justly and to love mercy and to walk humbly with your God (6: 6-8).

Micah called the people back to the basics, and his message is as relevant now as it was then. The prophecy ends with a psalm of praise, a tribute to the faithfulness of God to his covenant. God will turn again in mercy and compassion if his people will trust in him. And it is this promise which is the motivating force behind all prophetic preaching. To omit the promise is to omit the gospel.

> Who is a God like you, who pardons sin and forgives the transgression of the remnant of his inheritance? You do not stay angry forever but delight to show mercy. You will again have compassion on us; you will tread our sins underfoot and

hurl all our iniquities into the depths of the sea. You will be true to Jacob, and show mercy to Abraham, as you pledge on oath to our fathers in days long ago (7:18-20).

QUESTIONS FOR REFLECTION

1. What social sins does Micah condemn? Is sin purely an individual matter? Can sin be corporate? Is it possible to institutionalize sin?
2. How can one tell a false prophet from a true prophet? Do you think it is easy to distinguish them?
3. If Micah were to come to your church and speak about the "basics" of the religious life, what topics would he cover?
4. Does Micah's preaching have any significance for today?
5. What are the positive aspects of Micah's message?

CHAPTER 7

NAHUM

The Prophet of Comfort

Nahum was an Elkoshite from southwest Judah. Like many of the prophets, his personal identity lies in the obscurity of the past, but his message lives on in his prophecy and in the meaning of his name. Nahum means "comfort" and his poetic prediction of Nineveh's destruction was a consolation to the oppressed people of Judah who knew that "the Lord is good, a stronghold in the day of trouble, and he knows them who take refuge in him." (1:7). His prophecy reminds us of Isaiah 40:1-2"Comfort, comfort my people, says your God. Speak tenderly . . ."

Nahum is different from the other Minor Prophets in three respects. First, of all the twelve Minor Prophets this prophecy is called a "book" (1:1). Secondly, there is no condemnation of the sins of God's people, and thirdly, there is no call for repentance. The last two are the most commonly expected characteristics of the prophets but they are missing in Nahum. This gives us cause to refrain from stereotyping the prophets. The focus is rather on the evil city of Nineveh whose foreign policy had come into conflict with the will of God. In the context of Nineveh's inhuman cruelty and unspeakable atrocities, the prophet vindicates the nature of God.

JUDGMENT DECLARED (1:1-15)

Nahum begins his prophecy with a defense of God's character. As in our day, the prophet felt the need to deal with those who think God is uncaring in the face of so much evil. When God's people are suffering, they often question why God appears to tolerate injustice and ignore violations of basic human rights. The problem is especially acute if the righteous are oppressed by the wicked.

Nahum affirms certain attributes of God that we tend to overlook. C. S. Lewis once suggested that we seek, not so much a father in heaven, but a grandfather in heaven. Most people in the world like to think of God as a gentle old grandfather-type, who lets his grandchildren have the run of the house while he sits in the rocking chair with a "boys will be boys" smile on his face. We don't like to think of God as "jealous." Nahum of course does not mean that God is "the green-eyed monster." God does not lash out in vindictive, irrational anger when he doesn't get his way. When the Scripture speaks of God's anger or his wrath, it refers his judicial holiness in action against sin. When Nahum speaks of God being "jealous," he means that God demands total devotion, a holy exclusiveness which cannot tolerate rivals. The initial commandment in Exodus 20: 2-3 makes is crystal clear. "I am the Lord your God who has brought you out of the land of Egypt, out of the house of bondage. You shall have no other gods before me."

God hates idolatry, both in the church and in the world. There is no other God but God, and all lesser gods and their devotees will one day be destroyed. The Lord warned Nineveh: "I will destroy the carved images and cast idols that are in the temple of your gods. I will prepare your grave, for you are vile" (1:14).

The prophet sees the Lord as an "avenging" God, expressing holy wrath against all who oppose his will. He administers divine, deserved retribution for sins committed against his people. " 'Vengeance is mine; I will repay,' says the Lord" (Romans 12:19 RSV). Nahum is confident that God will vindicate this terrible injustice to his people and break the yoke from their necks and tear away their shackles (1:13). The announcement of Nineveh's fall and complete destruction was good news of long-awaited peace for the people of God (1:15).

> Look, there on the mountains, the feet of one who brings good news, who proclaims peace! Celebrate your festivals, O Judah, and fulfill your vows. No more will the wicked invade you; they will be completely destroyed (1:15).

JUDGMENT DESCRIBED (2:1-13)

The focus of the prophet's word was the city of Nineveh, the last capital city of Assyria. It was founded by Nimrod (Genesis 10: 11). Ancient historians tell us the high inner wall, which enclosed the city proper, had 1500 towers each 200 feet high, and was approximately 88 miles long and wide enough for 3 chariots to ride abreast on top of it. The population at the time of Nahum's prophecy may have been close to 200,000. It was, indeed, a great city in its day. Nineveh, however, was not so great in the eyes of God.

George L. Robinson wrote that Nineveh was "the capital of the most powerful, sensual, ferocious, and diabolically atrocious race of men that perhaps ever existed in all the world." Nahum and the people of Judah were powerless in the grasp of such an evil tyrant. The only comfort lay in the fact, twice repeated, that the Lord God had said, "Behold, I am against thee" (2:13, 3:5 KJV).

The prophet, seemingly in sarcasm, orders the Ninevites to prepare for battle: "An attacker advances against you, Nineveh. Guard the fortress, watch the road, brace yourselves, marshal all your strength!" (2:1).

The irony of it is the absolute uselessness of doing battle with God. If the Lord is for us, all is well. If the Lord is against us, who can be for us? The Lord was against Nineveh, and her destruction would be a devastating depletion of dramatic proportion.

The prophet describes the disaster in great detail. The palace collapses as the river gates are thrown open (2:6). Slave girls are screaming and moaning as the soldiers take gold and silver in their barbaric thirst for plunder and pillage. The evil, unmentioned by Nahum, leaves in its path melting hearts, weak knees, trembling bodies and horror-stricken faces (2:10).

Nahum's prophecy was fulfilled when Nineveh fell to the Medes and the Babylonians in 612 B.C. A sudden and unexpected overflowing of the Tigris River washed away part of the city wall and the foundation of the palace. The enemy armies entered through the breach and destroyed the city. The king, seeing that all was lost, set fire to the palace and he himself perished in the flames.

JUDGMENT DESERVED (3:1-19)

Nineveh's judgment was deserved. We should not think of God being merely a war monger who loves violence for violence sake. Remember that God is a just God with a just cause. Do forget, also, that the prophet Jonah had earlier witnessed Nineveh repent, but her repentance was short-lived and now she had relapsed into her former ungodly ways. We might say that Nineveh had overrun her line of credit with God, and the due date was upon her. The door of grace had closed. The flood of deserved judgment had arrived.

> Woe to the city of blood, full of lies, full of plunder, never

> without victims! The crack of whips, the clatter of wheels, galloping horses and jolting chariots! Charging cavalry, flashing swords and glittering spears! Many casualties, piles of dead, bodies without number, people stumbling over corpses—all because of the wanton lust of a harlot, alluring, the mistress of sorceries, who enslaved nations by her prostitution and peoples be her witchcraft. "I am against you," declares the Lord Almighty (3:1-5).

Nineveh's sins included plotting evil against the Lord and advocating wickedness (1:11). Assurbanipal, who captured the great Egyptian city of Thebes in 663 B.C. (3:8-10), was an unusually cruel ruler who boasted of his barbaric atrocities. Nahum called Nineveh "the city of blood" (3:1), referring, undoubtedly, to her murderous brutality and the war policies of their evil king. Nineveh had a policy of deceit. She was "full of lies" according to Nahum. Nineveh had no respect for human rights. She had a policy of greed and oppression. She was "full of plunder." Other sins of harlotry and witchcraft were predominant in the everyday life of the wicked city (3:4).

How can we limit the message of the prophet to Nineveh? We dare not! A visit to almost any corner store in North America will reveal that pornography and occult literature promote the same sins in our own day. The sections on Christianity in many respected bookstores are getting smaller and smaller while the shelves on paganism are getting longer and longer. The prophet's warning to Nineveh surely has a somber contemporary relevancy.

LEARNING FROM NAHUM

Is there anything we can learn from Nahum? Yes, several key lessons may be discovered. The people of God may take great comfort in the fact that the Lord is sovereign and in ultimate control of this world's affairs. There is someone who watches over us and is ever near us. We must take refuge in him alone (1:7).

Nineveh's security lay in the arm of flesh. Our security is in God. It is a great source of spiritual strength to know that God will one day right the wrongs of this world. We must not get discouraged when we see the wicked prosper while God's people seem to be destitute of worldly goods. We must, as it were, "keep the feasts and perform our vows" (1:15) because God will eventually destroy his enemies. Nineveh may be mighty, but God is almighty. God will settle the accounts in favor of his own people.

God will not allow sin to continue forever unpunished. There is a judgment day coming for all humankind. The Christian, whose sins were dealt with at Calvary, will still have to give an account at the judgment seat of Christ where his works will be tested and rewards handed out (2 Corinthians 5:10-11; 1 Corinthians 3:11-16).

The sinner who has refused to trust the atoning work of Christ's cross will meet him as the Judge at the Great White Throne judgment (Revelation 20:11-15), where the sentence of eternal damnation will be read. It is a doctrine no Christian can fine it joyful to believe. We believe it trembling and we preach it only with tears. No one need ever hear those solemn words, "Depart from me, ye workers of iniquity, into everlasting fire." No one need ever hear those words because hell was prepared for the devil and his angels. However, the Bible takes no pleasure in teaching that if we refuse Christ, we share in the devil's fate. There is only one way to avoid the Great White Throne judgment—the way of the old rugged cross.

The great pressure today is to recoil from this doctrine of hell and damnation. Even some evangelicals want to eliminate it from their teaching. They find it more tolerable to have a God who makes a real eternal heaven but a hell that is temporary or metaphorical. In that provocative work *The Problem of Pain*, C. S. Lewis writes that "the doors of hell are locked on the *inside*." God will give rebellious people what they ultimately desire and deserve. He will not override their wills. They get their own way in the end.

As Lewis suggested, there are really just two classes of people in the world; those who say to the Lord, "Thy will by done" and those to whom God says, "Thy will be done."

Many people, of course, downplay the Bible's teaching on hell, not because they are intentionally wicked people bent on deconstructing traditional dogmas. They are moved by the sheer enormity of the evangelistic task and the apparent impotence of the church in the face of it. They think the job of world missions is too big and the task force too small. It may be a great way to ease our conscience by postulating a secret plan of God to eliminate hell and provide salvation for all. It is tempting but we ought not to yield to such a temptation. It is too self-serving.

The people of God must keep the true nature of God before their eyes. We must never reduce God to some sentimental deity who is soft on sin. God will forgive any repented sin, but he will not turn a blind eye to it. If we invent such a God, we have not yet grasped the gravity of sin. Sin has to be repented of and forsaken. Paul in Romans 11:22 says, "Consider therefore the kindness and sternness of God: sternness to those who fell, but kindness to you, provided that you continue in his kindness. Otherwise, you also will be cut off." We must build our lives in the light of eternity and the true nature of God.

Like Nineveh, this world is headed for destruction (2 Peter 3: 10). Our only hope is that presently the day of grace has not ended and the call to repent and believe the gospel is still being heard in the land. However, we cannot be sure how long the message of the gospel will be offered. We do well to heed the old saying, "Only one life, 'twill soon be past. Only what's done for Christ will last."

QUESTIONS FOR REFLECTION

1. Why was God angry with Nineveh?
2. Is the rejoicing in Nahum 3:19 over the downfall of Nineveh incompatible with Christian attitudes?

3. Have you ever been in oppressive circumstances that seemed would last forever? What does Nahum have to teach us about this?
4. How do you think Nahum would react to the pornography plague in our society? How should Christians react?
5. Is God unconcerned about social injustice, racial prejudice and other human rights issues? What parts of Nahum give encouragement to the oppressed?
6. We raised the matter of eternal damnation in this chapter. Is this a moral doctrine?
7. Is it possible to be moral without the category of eternal damnation?
8. Do you think evangelicals are too "inward" in their approach to the gospel? Do we place too much emphasis on spiritual experience and too little on social impact? What is the relationship between inward and outward Christianity?

CHAPTER 8

Habakkuk

The Prophet with Questions

Habakkuk deals with the hard questions. His piety is not superficial and he is not content with pat answers. To some, his honest and direct complaining to God would appear impious and rude. The prophet was concerned with the specific problem of unanswered prayer and the classic difficulty posed by the apparent triumph of evil in a world where the sovereign God is strangely silent. Habakkuk's prophecy, therefore, is a theodicy, that is, a justification of the complex ways of God. It is this theological theme which is of paramount importance in the book.

About Habakkuk, himself, very little is known. Most conservative scholars identify him as a prophet who wrote during the reign of Jehoiakim (612-587 B.C.). He is designated as "a prophet," which may be defined as a person who, by inspiration, received "oracles" or "burdens" from God for the edification and exhortation of God's people. The soul of this prophet was troubled. He was sensitive to the sin and evil and he reasoned earnestly with God, whom he knew to be omnipotent. Why was the almighty God, who was able to deal with sin and evil, so long in answering prayer? Why was God silent?

Habakkuk's problem was created by certain presuppositions which he held about the nature of God. If these were untrue, there would be no problem. He believed God to be the all-powerful sovereign Creator and Sustainer of the world. Therefore he ought to be able to stamp out evil. After all, the Almighty is not an impotent deity but an omnipotent God. He believed that God was holy, righteous and just. Therefore he should want to stamp out evil. He also believed that evil was real. If God were not sovereign, almighty, holy, righteous and just, or if evil were merely an illusion, there would be no problem. But, God is almighty and all loving and, yet, evil abounds. It's a big problem with no easy solution, not even for the one who prays.

THE PROPHET'S FIRST COMPLAINT (1:2-4)

The prophet's anguish broke out in a prayer of exasperation. "O Lord, how long shall I cry for help, and thou wilt not hear?" Like many of us when we pray, he was lamenting because his prayer was not swiftly answered. He wanted to see action right away. He wanted to hear from the Lord, but the heavens were as brass. He implored God to deal with the situation, but no action came. As a result of the silence of God, many people at the time resorted to a practical atheism and were in a backslidden condition. Wickedness prevailed in the land, the law was paralyzed and justice perverted. It was not an easy time to be a prophet. It never is!

Habakkuk's problem was not his alone. All the prophets shared the same perplexity. Indeed, every true believer wrestles with events that seem to be irreconcilable with God's sovereignty. Why does God allow the world to go its own merry way? Why does God seem to put off answering prayer, right to the last minute? How can God remain silent while the righteous are oppressed, the wicked prosper, right and wrong are disregarded, God himself insulted and the world goes to hell in a hand-basket? Have you not asked similar questions yourself?

GOD'S RESPONSE (1:5-11)

Sometimes God's answers are more disconcerting than his silence. Such is the case here. God informed Habakkuk that he was, indeed, about his business, although not in the way the prophet expected or desired! The one who prays must resist the temptation to give God an agenda for answering prayer. His ways are above our ways and incredibly mysterious.

God often uses unexpected means to accomplish his purposes. God told Habakkuk that he was raising up the Chaldeans to execute judgment on the people of God. This greatly feared people marched forward with a reign of terror in their wake. They acknowledged no law but themselves, and nothing could withstand them. It is ironic how God used those whose justice proceeded from themselves to punish those who perverted the justice which proceeded from God.

This sovereign activity of God was unanticipated and perplexing to the prophet. Yet the people of God could take encouragement from knowing that the Lord was still on the throne. He was the one who raised up the Chaldeans. They were a whip in the hand of God. Undoubtedly they would give the credit for their success to their own prowess; nevertheless, God is the Lord of history, and all events are under his sovereign control. It was not an easy thing to believe, but the alternative is out of the question. God is in control and when he is done with the whip he will discard it.

THE PROPHET'S SECOND COMPLAINT (1:12-17)

Habakkuk apparently was unsatisfied with God's answer because he thought it conflicted with God's character. How could a holy God use such unholy people like the Chaldeans as a means of punishing his covenant family? Why would God use a nation less righteous than Judah to punish Judah? The prophet's questions were cradled in the positive affirmations of faith. Yet these questions plagued the prophet, and their deep emotional effect on him can be readily seen in these verses. It was a faith whose companion was a heaviness of heart. Strong faith and deep honest questions are not incompatible.

God had not answered as Habakkuk expected. The prophet had to learn that the Almighty was not a vending machine which delivers the desired goods because of the proper amount of "nickel and dime" prayers placed in the slot. Praying is not like rubbing an Aladdin's lamp. God does not operate like a self-appointed wonderworker who dazzles the crowds by the dramatic pseudo miraculous. He does not accept the policy of being an instant cure-all for our perplexities. It is true that God is the God of miracles. However, God may unfold his answers to our prayers in ways that are strange and complicated. We must rest confident that he is in sovereign control, even when he appears not to be.

Honest doubts such as those which distressed the prophet may be evidence of a strong faith, not a weak faith. Faith which faces no adversity can hardly be faith at all. True faith is tempered in the fires of hard questions and difficult situations (cf. Hebrews 11).

> In this you greatly rejoice, though now for a little while you may have had to suffer grief in all kinds of trials. These have come so that your faith—of greater worth than gold, which perishes even though refined by fire—may be proved genuine and may result in praise, glory and honor when Jesus Christ is revealed (1 Peter 1:6-7).

In 1:12 Habakkuk writes, "We will not die." This is a strong statement of faith in God's faithfulness. He will not break his word. No matter how dark the skies, God will not abandon his chosen people. The Chaldeans may do whatever they wish, but they cannot totally destroy the elect of God.

For the Christian going through the deep waters of sorrow, sickness or economic adversity, there is an uplifting word here. "Though he fall, he shall not be utterly cast down" (Psalm 37:24 KJV). We can depend on God's faithfulness. Though the state of affairs go from bad to worse, as in the case of Habakkuk, our God does not change. On that we can rely.

Habakkuk was living in that difficult time between the prayer and the answer, between the promise and the fulfillment. This is where faith is really needed.

GOD'S SECOND RESPONSE (2:1-5)

God told Habakkuk to write the vision on tablets, which would give the message permanence and secure the future remembrance of the prophecy. It was to be written plainly so that the passerby could read it with ease.

The message was that, despite all evidence to the contrary, wickedness and injustice will not last forever. The righteous will endure and they will live by faith (2:4). This verse is used by Paul in Romans 1:17 to teach the heart of the Christian gospel, justification by faith.

The righteous are those who remain faithful in times when faith doesn't seem to make any sense or bring instant solutions. Faith is not always measured by success or positive answers to our prayers. Indeed, faith is measured by faithfulness.

In our evangelical world, where the "prosperity gospel" is making health and wealth the measure of faith, many less fortunate Christians (and those who have literally forsaken all to follow Jesus) are cruelly derided by mistaken charlatans as having little faith. Much of this teaching is a result of (1) an unbiblical understanding of faith, (2) an improper interpretation of the Scriptures, (3) an attempt to justify our materialism (try preaching in the streets of Calcutta), and (4) an overrealized eschatology, that is, attempting to realize in our present experience what God has promised for the future.

It is true that many Christians live below their privileges, yet some have been known to claim that they already have their resurrection bodies and they will never die! They think that in a certain level of praise they can miss that appointment with death. But until the trumpet sounds and the rapture of the church takes place, we will all become victims to the last enemy. However, we have the promise that the dead in Christ shall rise, and we shall! True faith endures the difficult period between the prayer and the answer. Some things will be ours only in the prophetic future. True faith doesn't demand now what God has reserved for later. The wise Christian is a patient Christian.

THE FIVE WOES (2:6-20)

After the great statement, that the righteous will live by faith and trust in the faithfulness of God, the woes in chapter 2 seem to be rather anticlimactic. However, they are designed to show us that the triumph of evil in the world is only apparent. There is no cause for depression. In the long term God's sovereign purpose will prevail. The plundering Chaldeans will be plundered (2:6-8). Their ambitious schemes will crumble (2:9-11). Their cities built by sin will be destroyed (2:12-14). The depraved ones will be brought low (2:15-17). Idol worship will be shown up for the farce that it is (2:18-19).

The woes end with an exhortation: "But the Lord is in his holy temple; let all the earth be silent before him" (2:20). There is irony in this verse. Habakkuk had complained about the silence of God earlier. God, now, appears to be concerned about the lack of silence upon the earth. We cannot dictate to God. We cannot write him into our lives as some author who determines the part his characters will play. We must be submissive to his will because, despite apparent evidence to the contrary, God is on the throne; he is still in his holy temple.

THE PROPHET'S POETIC PRAYER (3:1-19)

The final chapter of the book is a poetic composition which some scholars think may have been used in Jewish liturgical worship. It is an intercessory prayer, probably designed to be sung. Habakkuk prays that God will remember to be merciful in wrath (3:2). He describes God as a great warrior with thunder and lightning surrounding him, against whom nothing can stand or impede his progress (3:3-7). This mighty God comes for two reasons: to save his people and to execute judgment upon their enemies (3: 8-15). The enemies are represented by rivers, mountains, waters and seas.

The closing paragraph is the most famous expression of faith in the entire Bible. The great manifestation of the power of the Almighty caused the prophet to tremble, and he pledged to be patient in the midst of impending doom. Habakkuk has learned not to base his theology on circumstances, whether good or bad.

> Though the fig tree does not bud and there are no grapes on the vines, though the olive crop fails and the fields produce no food, though there are no sheep in the pen and no cattle in the stalls, yet I will rejoice in the Lord, I will be joyful in God my Savior. The Sovereign Lord is my strength (3:17-19).

The silence of God between the prayer and the answer is insufficient reason to abandon faith, though all evidence may point to failure. The fig tree, the grapevines and the farm may be unproductive. The cattle may be dying. Our situation may be that of the starving thousands in the Third World. Yet the people of God must realize that God has not changed; he has not forsaken his people. The evil in the world will eventually be judged. In that knowledge we can rejoice in the God who is our strength. Living between the prayer and the answer isn't easy, but, as Spurgeon once said, "We must trust where we cannot trace."

QUESTIONS FOR REFLECTION

1. Habakkuk felt free to question God's methods and timing in answering prayer. What does this indicate about his relationship with God?
2. Make a list of the specific sins which the prophet condemns. What effects do these sins have on the sinner and on others?
3. What application of Habakkuk 2:4 does Paul make in Galatians 3:11?
4. What should be the attitude of Christians suffering under oppressive governments and/or situations?
5. Does Habakkuk view human history in a positive or negative way? Explain.
6. What may we learn from Habakkuk about dealing with the problem of evil?

CHAPTER 9

Zephaniah

The End Times Prophet

As they stand in our Bible, the twelve Minor Prophets may be divided into two groups. The first nine, of which Zephaniah is the last in order, ministered before the exile in Babylon. Although Habakkuk was actually the last pre-exilic prophet, Zephaniah is placed last in order because his message sums up the major themes of the other pre-exilic prophets. The remaining three Minor Prophets yet to be considered, Haggai, Zechariah and Malachi, ministered after the exile and are therefore called the post-exilic prophets.

The genealogy, which goes back four generations, in the opening verse of the book, indicates that the prophet Zephaniah had royal blood. His great-great-grandfather was the godly King Hezekiah who had found favor in the eyes of the Lord. Zephaniah wrote his prophecy about 625 B.C., after he received the word of the Lord during the reign of Josiah over Judah (640-609 B.C.). In 2 Kings chapters 22 and 23, we learn that a great reform had taken place during the reign of Josiah but, because no mention of it occurs in this prophecy, it is likely that Zephaniah preached before the reform. Indeed, it is possible his preaching contributed to the reform.

Zephaniah was a man of such moral sensitivity, godly passion and strong convictions about sin that he often sounds improperly harsh and condemnatory. He spoke with boldness and courage. Nevertheless, he was not a pessimist. His spirituality was profoundly positive as he spoke a message of judgment yet looked forward to the restoration of Judah's fortunes (2:7, 3:20).

His prophecy of three short chapters contains a timeless and timely message for the church today. Chapter 1:1-18 introduces the theme of the day of the Lord and its judgment upon Judah. First, God will deal with sinful leaders among his people who treat people with "violence and deceit" (1:9). He will punish the complacent and the wealthy (1:12-18). How this will be done is not clearly stated but the images of "warrior," "trumpet" and "battle cry" give some intimation of the method God will use. Chapter 2:1-15 extends the application of divine wrath to other nations: Philistia, Moab, Ammon, Cush and Assyria. They will experience his anger; they will be plundered for "insulting and mocking the people of the Lord Almighty" (2:10). Chapter 3:1-20 declares, for a second time, woe upon Jerusalem, and the final vindication and exaltation of God's people with celebration and joy.

THE WARNING TO JUDAH

Zephaniah wasted no time in getting right to the point: God was about to judge his people (1:2-4). Judah's situation was very bleak spiritually. The people were callous and indifferent; worldliness abounded. It was time for God to act. Twenty-two times in the book God says, "I will," showing that his judgment agenda is about to begin.

God warned Judah because of her sins. She was guilty of idolatry. She tolerated and participated in the worship of the planets and the pagan gods Baal and Molech (1:4-5). Judah was guilty of religious syncretism, that unholy mixture of the true worship of Jehovah and paganism (1:5). That sin exists today in many different forms such as the mixture of Jesus and Transcendental Meditation, Jesus and the horoscope, Jesus and the world, Jesus and Gaia, etc. Many forms of modern Baalism are evident today and even advocated by some writers. Also, Judah was guilty of the sin of indifference (1:6). Undoubtedly this resulted in their absence from the true place of worship and prayer, the neglect of financial support for the Lord's work, the tolerance of secret sins and the blatant disobedience of God's ethical commands. Apathy is a deadening of the soul that is hard to reverse once started. It is spiritually lethal.

Judah had assimilated the surrounding culture and had accommodated to the world. The reference to "foreign clothes" in 1:8 most likely refers to those who imitated the pagan priests in their religious garb, or it may refer to their extravagant interests in keeping abreast of the latest foreign fashions. Judah was adopting religious and social customs which were unacceptable to God. She had ceased to be a unique people (Exodus 33:16). She had conformed to the world (cf. Romans 12:2). Judah had also bowed down to idols and held to superstitions. The reference to "stepping on the threshold" (1:9) probably refers to the pagan belief that evil spirits lived on the doorsteps of houses. Our custom of carrying the bride over the threshold has its roots in that superstitious belief. Apparently God does not take kindly to superstitious practices.

Judah had departed so far from the covenant laws that justice was forgotten and in its place violence and fraud ruled the day (1:9). Judah felt she had to play ball with the world. She wanted acceptance. Compromise, tolerance and peaceful coexistence characterized the attitude of God's people. The laws of their invisible God no longer seemed relevant.

The Christian church faces similar temptations. In our efforts to be realistic and relevant we look at the Bible as an old book, written to other people, another culture, another time. We have to be up-to-date, do we not? We argue and we compromise. We cut the cloth of the gospel to fit the modern person. We seek to justify the gospel before a sinful humanity when we should be seeking to justify sinful humanity before the gospel as Dietrich Bonhoeffer once suggested.

We desire acceptance with the unacceptable crowd. As a result, we cheapen the message, offering a substitute remedy and not the proper cure. Bonhoeffer challenges the church to offer "costly grace" instead of "cheap grace," which he defines as

> the justification of the sin without the justification of the sinner. . . the preaching of forgiveness without requiring repentace, baptism without church discipline, communion without confession, absolution without personal confession. Cheap grace is grace without discipleship, grace without the cross, grace without Jesus Christ, living and incarnate (*Cost of Discipleship*, pp. 35-36).

The prophet called Judah a "shameless nation" (2:1). Judah had ceased being ashamed of her sins. She had gone so far as to desensitize her conscience. Loss of shame and coldness of heart are sure signs of a backslidden condition. We need a recovery of a sense of shame in our times because we have stopped feeling disgraced by our sin. True repentance is accompanied by a genuine sense of shame and humility of soul. C. S. Lewis said in *The Problem of Pain* that if the Christian faith is true the view of ourselves that "we have in moments of shame must be the only true view." The newsstands and movie industry testify that ours, too, is a shameless nation, and the soul of any righteous person can be nothing else but vexed by the loss of shame in our society.

Zephaniah sums up the situation in the first chapter. The people say, "The Lord will not do good, nor will he do ill" (v.12 RSV). Theirs was a convenient agnosticism. Sin had so dulled their minds that God's existence had no practical significance. If he did exist, he was as impotent as the idols. He was merely one god among many, and just as useless.

THE DAY OF THE LORD

Only a radical solution would work. The prophet thundered, "Be silent before the Lord God! For the day of the Lord is at hand" (1:7 RSV). The day of the Lord would change their minds.

Zephaniah is the most descriptive of the prophets in his treatment of the day of the Lord (1:7-13). It is a day that is near, he claims. It is fast approaching. It is the day of the Lord's anger and wrath against the enemies of his people. It is a day of gloom and darkness. It is a day of battles.

The day of the Lord is a major theme in Christian eschatology. In New Testament prophecy, the concept is usually referred to as "the time of Jacob's trouble" or the great tribulation, the awful judgment which will come upon the earth before the second coming of Christ to establish his millennial reign. The only way to escape that terrible day is to trust in Christ alone for salvation. He is the only refuge (1 Thessalonians 5:9).

The prophet's call was for a solemn assembly, a period of seeking the Lord. He called for humility, obedience and righteousness before the Lord. Only a repentance that is truly genuine will bring protection in the day of the Lord's wrath.

The prophet spoke a word of woe to the sinful nations. He said, "The word of the Lord is against you" (2:5). What an awful indictment! Unless the world repents of its sins and turns to God, only divine anger awaits it.

The prophet also spoke a word of woe to the city of Jerusalem, too. That city was to uphold the holy standards of God but tolerated evil in high places. The accusations are dreadful:

> Woe to the city of oppressors, rebellious and defiled! She obeys no one, she accepts no correction. She does not trust in the Lord, she does not draw near to her God. Her officials are roaring lions; her rulers are evening wolves, who leave nothing for the morning. Her prophets are arrogant; they are treacherous men. Her priests profane the sanctuary and do violence to the law (3:1-5).

The holy city turned out to be very unholy. The very place where holiness ought to be seen was, instead, a place reeking of unrighteousness. How serious it is to carry God's name but in our behavior dishonor that name. Such behavior is a form of taking the name of our Lord in vain, a breaking of one of the Ten Commandments. God's people must not take God's grace for granted. Having the "name" of "Christian" will not prove to be a good-luck charm in the day of the Lord. God will confront sin with judgment wherever he finds it, not only in the world, but also in the church. May we not say, especially in the church?

God's people were without excuse. God had sought to bring his people to their spiritual senses in several ways (3:1-8). He had given them his covenant laws, but they refused to obey them. He was faithful but they were unfaithful. He had destroyed their enemies, but they had not seen the warnings to themselves inherent in God's actions. They continued to "make all their deeds corrupt," according to the prophet (3:7 RSV). Judah had rejected all the guidelines, therefore God will act in judgment.

FUTURE HOPE

All is not dark, though, in this prophecy. The grace of God can still be seen, and it is expressed in several faith-inspiring promises. As Zephaniah looked to the future, he saw a ray of hope. The people who seek the Lord will be protected in the great day of the Lord's anger (2:3). The remnant of the house of Judah will settle in peaceful coastlands (2:7), and they will get the better of their foes (2:9). A great revival will happen, with many people turning to the Lord (3:9). The proud will be taken away and wickedness will cease forever, he says (3:11-12). The King of Israel, the Lord, will be in the midst of his people. He will rejoice over them with gladness and their fortunes will be restored in a future time of joyful celebration (3:15, 20).

The day of the Lord is a dark theme in Zephaniah, as in the other prophets. However, one positive thing can be said about the day of the Lord. It is still future. It has not happened yet. This means that the day of grace has not ended. It's not too late to return to God. The situation is not hopeless. The door of mercy has not closed. Christ, who has died on the cross of Calvary, has suffered the day of the Lord for all who come to him in faith and repentance. We need not experience the wrath of that day. Christ has died for us and for our salvation. That is what the Christian faith proclaims. It is good news, news that we ought to accept and believe. It is the content of the call of the gospel. Repent and believe the good news. Salvation is possible.

One thinks of the great conclusion to Peter's sermon on the day of Pentecost in Acts 2:37-40.

> Peter said, "Change your life. Turn to God and be baptized, each of you, in the name of Jesus Christ, so your sins are forgiven. Receive the gift of the Holy Spirit. The promise is targeted to you and your children, but also to all who are far away--whomever, in fact, our Master God invites." He went on in this vein for a long time, urging them over and over, "Get out while you can; get out of this sick and stupid culture!" (*The Message*)

Peter sounded much like the prophet and, indeed, the call in Zephaniah 2:3 is still the only escape:

Seek the Lord, all you humble of the land, you who do what he commands. Seek righteousness, seek humility; perhaps you will be sheltered on the day of the Lord's anger.

QUESTIONS FOR REFLECTION

1. What complaints did Zephaniah have against the religious establishment of his day?
2. We have said that God doesn't take kindly to superstitious practices. In what ways are modern people superstitious? Is it evident in the church?
3. Using a concordance, look up the word *remnant* in all the prophets. What are the characteristics of those who compose the remnant of God's people?
4. Highlight or underline the number of times "I will" occurs. What does this say about the involvement of God in human affairs?
5. How does Zephaniah describe the day of the Lord? How does his description compare with that of the other Minor Prophets?
6. How is the mercy and grace of God evident in Zephaniah's prophecy?

CHAPTER 10

Haggai

The Temple Builder

Haggai, along with Zechariah and Malachi, make up the three post-exilic prophets who prophesied in Judah after the seventy-year exile in Babylon. Haggai's prophecy is not disputed regarding the date. All agree on a date of about 520 B.C. The prophet's name, which means "festal one," probably suggests that he was born on a feast day. Although very little is known of him personally, the historical context of his message is to be found in the book of Ezra that relates the struggle faced by the people of Judah after certain exiles returned from the captivity in Babylon.

> When the builders laid the foundation of the temple of the Lord, the priests in their vestments and with trumpets, and the Levites (the sons of Asaph) with cymbals, took their places to praise the Lord, as prescribed by David king of Israel. With praise and thanksgiving they sang to the Lord: "He is good; his love to Israel endures forever." And all the people gave a great shout of praise to the Lord, because the foundation of the house of the Lord was laid (Ezra 3:10-11).

> Then the peoples around them set out to discourage the people of Judah and make them afraid to go on building. They hired counselors to work against them and frustrate their plans (Ezra 4:4-5).

> Thus the work on the house of God in Jerusalem came to a standstill (Ezra 4:24).

Three groups of God's people had been taken into captivity—in 605 B.C., 597 B.C. and 586 B.C. Three groups had also returned—in 538 B.C. and 458 B.C. under Ezra and in 445 B.C. under Nehemiah. The background to the message of Haggai may be summarized in this way. The remnant, "the cream of the crop" spiritually, had returned from the Babylonian captivity. They had been political prisoners who had survived and now were united in purpose and perspective. They were a worshipping community, intent on the reinstitution of the feasts and restoring the altar that had fallen into disrepair. They were a hard-working community and they set about to rebuild the temple. They had even succeeded in completing the laying of the foundation. However, the work had come grinding to a halt because of opposition from the neighboring peoples and because of an attitude of indifference that had settled in among the people of God.

In such a context, the prophet Haggai faced two major problems. First, the temple of God was uncompleted, basically in ruins, and secondly, the people of God seemed content to leave it that way. They had lapsed into apathy. They were satisfied to give to God what was left over in their lives. As far as time was concerned, they gave to the Lord's work only what they would spare after taking care of their own personal interests. Their priorities were not straight, and the prophet was quite concerned about it. His word to them, and to us, is to consider our ways, take courage and work! Four messages are evident in the book, each beginning with the words, "The word of the Lord came through the prophet Haggai."

THE FIRST MESSAGE (1:1-15)

The first message (1:1-15) was addressed to the governor and the high priest. It was really a note of accusation. Haggai saw the neglect of the temple as the cause of the economic hardship experienced by the people.

> The word of the Lord came through the prophet Haggai: "Is it a time for you yourselves to be living in your paneled houses, while this house remains a ruin?" Now this is what the Lord Almighty says: "Give careful thought to your ways. You have planted much, but have harvested little. You eat, but never have enough. You drink, but never have your fill. You put on clothes, but are not warm. You earn wages, only to put them in a purse with holes in it" (1:3-6).

The original reason why the restoration work had stopped was opposition from an external source. But now, the cause was more internal than external. The people of God were caught up in the "legitimate enterprises" of planning and building, buying and selling. The cares of this world and the deceitfulness of riches were choking their spiritual vitality. The prophet did not rant against a long catalogue of big sins like adultery and idolatry. The people were involved in the sin of a false contentment with "all these things" rather than seeking "first the kingdom of God and his righteousness." Haggai faced the difficult problem of motivating an apathetic congregation.

When God's people are not doing what they are called to do, the minister of the Lord faces the particular temptation to be harsh and condemnatory. At such times it is easy for the pastor to make the mistake of screaming and yelling about "lazy" Christians. But Haggai's pastoral methodology shows a much wiser approach.

Haggai first calls the people to consider their ways. The phrase "give careful thought" occurs five times in the prophecy (1:5, 7;

2:15, 18). He urges them to do a proper inward inventory. God's people were living in relative luxury while God's house lay in ruins. They had been working at it for more than a decade and it still wasn't finished. They had allowed the legitimate pressures of life to take priority. As a result, they were not receiving the full blessings of God. They were planting seed but not reaping the full harvest which the Lord intended. They were earning money only to discover that their purses were full of holes. The lifestyle and the thought patterns of the world had robbed them of spiritual blessings.

Haggai's second approach was to appeal to the people on the basis of God's glory. God's glory refers not merely to his brightness but also his reputation. The honor and reputation of God would be enhanced if the work on the temple restarted. The neighboring people, at that time, associated the greatness of gods with the kind of building erected in their honor. To build a great building would be to enhance the reputation of one's god. Therefore, a temple lying in ruins dishonored God in the eyes of the surrounding nations. In such circumstances the testimony of God's people was nullified. It isn't much good to say words of praise to God if what one builds in honor of God reflects something else. Symbols often speak louder than human voices. To the onlookers, the obvious statement being made by their neglect in temple restoration was that the returned exiles did not take their religion seriously and did not consider their God worthy of their best.

It is impossible to resist the critique of some postmodern forms of church architecture. Rather than building churches around a "sanctuary" devoted to proclamation, sacraments and worship, many groups of Christians opt for a multipurpose complex consisting of a gymnasium, kitchen and offices. There is no sacred worship space dedicated to the glory of God. It is replaced by a gymnasium devoid of symbol and art serving as a meeting place dedicated to fun, fellowship and food. One wonders what Haggai would say.

Of course, one could respond that God dwells in our hearts and not in a physical temple. And, we would have to agree. However, I have a sneaky feeling that Haggai didn't take that approach. He didn't say, "It doesn't matter what the temple looks like; it's what's in your heart that counts!" We have to be careful with such trite iconoclastic responses or we will make an unnecessary dichotomy between the Old and New Testaments and treat the prophets as irrelevant or archaic. There is no higher motive for Christian service than to glorify God. Our good works done in the right spirit, although they cannot save us, show to the people of the world the glory of God. As Jesus said in Matthew, "Let your light so shine before all people, that they may see your good works and glorify your Father who is in heaven."

As a result of the prophet's wise approach to the problems he faced, a remnant of the people obeyed the voice of God and the message of the prophet.

> "Then Zerubbabel the son of Shealtiel, and Joshua the son of Josedech, the high priest, with all the remnant of the people, obeyed the voice of the LORD their God, and the words of Haggai the prophet, as the LORD their God had sent him, and the people did fear before the LORD. Then spake Haggai the LORD'S messenger in the LORD'S message unto the people, saying, I am with you, saith the LORD" (1:12-13 KJV).

It is interesting to note the close relationship between the prophet's message and the voice of God. The people did not become angry but took Haggai's exhortation to heart. They responded with faith and action, and Haggai assured them that God would be with them.

There is an encouraging word here. When God makes demands on us, as he has the right to do, he promises us, not only strength for the task but his presence also. God's will is never an agenda that we must accomplish alone. God is present with us in the work to which he calls us. The promises of the covenant are true. "I will be with you. You will be my people." This, too, is a powerful motive for Christian service. Whether our lot is suffering or success, pain or pleasure, the promise of God's presence is a great source of power, strength, holy boldness, comfort and encouragement. The first message ends with the Lord stirring up the spirit of the whole remnant (1:14).

THE SECOND MESSAGE (2:1-9)

The second message (2:1-9) was directed against a false discontent. After the people had started to work, there arose a fear that they would not be able to match the splendor of Solomon's temple. They became discouraged. They were comparing the beauty and glory of the former temple with their own meager efforts. They were comparing their weaknesses to Solomon's strengths. They were using a false standard. The prophet encouraged them to be strong in the Lord, to realize the Lord's presence and to work hard. God would bless their faithful labor. God's people must not use their lack of talents or gifts as excuses for complaining. Faithfulness in small things will always bring the approval of God.

Haggai wanted the remnant to be aware that their work was fulfilling the promise of the covenant made during the exodus. No matter how little it seemed, the work had significance. Because the Spirit of the Lord remained with them, they were assured of ultimate success. "'The glory of this present house will be greater than the glory of the former house,' says the Lord Almighty" (2: 9). The second message ends with what appears to be a messianic passage. The Lord will shake the heavens and the earth, and all nations and the desired of nations will come.

THE THIRD MESSAGE (2:10-19)

The third message (2:10-19) makes clear that moral uncleanness is easily transferred, but moral cleanness is personal. For example, the common cold is easily communicated from one child to another, but health is not. Haggai's point is that ungodliness in the people contaminates the sacrifices. God desires his people to give careful thought to this. But now that the work on the temple had restarted, God would again bless his people. "From this day on I will bless you." God, who withheld the blessings, would again sovereignly bestow them.

THE FOURTH MESSAGE (2:20-23)

The prophet ends his prophecy with a promise of ultimate and final triumph. This prophecy is directed to Zerubbabel, the governor. God promises to shake the nations and the whole created order, and the governor is to be made like God's signet ring, a symbol of great authority. Some commentators see this passage as messianic. The messianic line was to come through Zerubbabel as well as David. In the light that Zerubbabel was an ancestor of the Lord Jesus, this interpretation is possible. It appears that the governor was to be elevated to a position of high honor "on that day."

From the prophet Haggai we learn that we cannot give to God the leftovers of our energy and efforts. God ought not to be penciled into our agenda after we have scheduled everything else. We must endeavor to be totally committed to the Lord's work. We have to take frequent, deep-searching inventories of our lives in order to prevent the world from shaping us. We learn that God is a great motivator and we are missing out on many spiritual blessings if we are unconcerned about his will. We also learn that no matter how little it seems, God is present with us in our work for him, and our labor is never in vain in the Lord.

QUESTIONS FOR REFLECTION

1. Do you think it was easy to be a prophet in Haggai's context? Imagine that Haggai asks you to pray for his ministry. What needs would he share with you?
2. Note the number of times "Give careful thought" (NIV) or "Consider your ways" (KJV) occurs in the prophecy. What does this indicate about the importance of self-examination?
3. Do pastors find similar problems in congregation today as Haggai found among the people of God in his day?
4. What parts of Haggai's message do you find most convicting? What are you going to do about it? What parts do you find most comforting?
5. Would Haggai be for or against Christians investing heavily in real estate during a church building program? Would his attitude change of the church's mortgage were paid?

CHAPTER 11

ZECHARIAH

The Prophet of Messiah

More than two dozen men in the Bile have the name Zechariah, which means "the Lord remembers." The Scripture indicates that Iddo, Zachariah's grandfather, was of the priestly tribe (Nehemiah 12:4, 16), which suggests that this Zechariah may have been a priest as well as a prophet.

The prophet Zechariah was a contemporary of Haggai (Ezra 6: 14) and his message is similar. Like Haggai, he writes to encourage those who returned from the Babylonian captivity and who had settled in and around the site of the city of Jerusalem. Temple reconstruction had started but was still incomplete. The people were somewhat depressed because their efforts at temple building did not compare with the splendor of Solomon's temple (Ezra 3: 12). Therefore the prophet sought to uplift the drooping faith of God's people and motivate the discouraged remnant into restarting the work of temple restoration (Zechariah 4:10).

The prophecy begins with a call to confession and repentance. "This is what the Lord Almighty says: 'Return to me,' declares the Lord Almighty, 'and I will return to you," says the Lord Almighty" (1:3).

Zechariah's message is more messianic that Haggai's. Being concerned about the insincerity of many of those who had returned, he exhorts them to repent of their sin and to return wholeheartedly to the Lord. The motive for returning to the Lord was that the Lord had not forgotten them and that he was at work in their midst, preparing them for the coming of Messiah, the one who would restore to Israel her spiritual inheritance.

The book of Zechariah, the longest of the Minor Prophets, is considered by many commentators to be the most difficult to interpret. Three basic divisions may be seen in the book: the first, chapters 1-6, contains eight visions; the second, chapters 7-8, contains four short messages; and the third, chapters 9-14, contain two longer oracles.

THE EIGHT VISIONS

The first section contains the eight prophetic visions which disclose several important truths about Israel's future that dispel discouragement and despair. There is a glorious future for the people of God because Messiah will come. There will be ultimate victory for Israel over her enemies. There will be a world-wide messianic kingdom, with the anointed one reigning as king.

The first vision of the person among the myrtle trees with red, brown and whites horses (1:1-17) symbolizes the care of God for his people and his intention to insure the rebuilding of the temple and the prosperity of Israel (vv. 16-17).

In the second vision (1:18-21), the four horns represent the nations that scattered Israel, while the four craftsmen represent those by whom Israel's enemies will meet their ultimate destruction.

The third vision, the man with the measuring line (2:1-13), illustrates the expansion of Jerusalem in future days because of the blessing of God.

The fourth, the vision of Joshua the high priest (3:1-10) being separated from his filthy clothes and reclothed in clean garments is one of the most explicit and beautiful illustrations of the doctrine of justification by faith in the whole of Scripture. Filthy, sin-stained garments disqualify one from the priestly service of God. As revelation progressively unfolds we learn that through faith in the sacrifice of Christ, the Lamb of God, those sins stains are covered by his righteous robes. Another picture in the New Testament is that our garments are washed in the blood of the Lamb. This vision of Zechariah also points to the future cleansing of Israel when her iniquity is taken away and "all Israel will be saved" (Romans 11: 26).

The fifth vision of the lampstand and olive trees (4:1-14) portrays Israel in her role of dispensing light under the rule of Messiah. It also declares that the Spirit of God will be present in a special way in the last days. God brings his plans to fruition, "not by might nor by power, but by my Spirit," says the Lord Almighty.

The sixth vision, the flying scroll (5:1-4), teaches that God will destroy the wicked from the land, while the seventh vision, the woman sitting in the measuring basket (5:5-11) symbolizes the removal of sin.

The final vision of the four chariots (6:1-8) represents the carrying out of divine judgment against the nations. The visions end with the crowning of the high priest which, undoubtedly, is a symbol of the crowning of Christ as King of Kings and Lord of Lords.

FOUR SHORTER MESSAGES

The second section of Zechariah, chapters 7-8, proclaims four shorter messages. The first (7:1-7) condemns empty ritual. God is not impressed by fasting when the important social elements of the spiritual life are neglected:

> This is what the Lord Almighty says: "Administer true justice; show mercy and compassion to one another. Do not oppress the widow or the fatherless, the alien or the poor. In your hearts do not think evil of each other" (7:8-10).

The second short message (7:8-14) contains warnings, based on the past judgments of God, against ignoring the word of the prophets:

> They made their hearts as hard as flint and would not listen to the law or to the words the Lord Almighty had sent by his Spirit through the earlier prophets. So the Lord Almighty was very angry (7:12).

The third message (8:1-19) promises a future restoration of the nation of Israel, when fasting will give way to feasting. This is what the Lord Almighty says: "I will save my people . . ." (8:7).

> The seed will grow well, the vine will yield its fruit, the ground will produce its crops, and the heaven will drop their dew. I will give all these things as an inheritance to the remnant of this people. As you have been the object of cursing among the nations, O Judah and Israel, so I will save you and you will be a blessing. Do not be afraid, but let your hands be strong (8:12-13).

The fourth message (8:2-23) promises a future and worldwide acceptance of the Lord of Hosts.

TWO LONG ORACLES

The third division of the book, chapter 9-14, is composed of two longer burdens, or "oracles." Chapters 9-11 deal with the first advent of Messiah and his rejection. This section contains a great deal of messianic prophecy which Christians see as fulfilled in the life and death of Jesus. Chapters 12-14 concern the second advent of Messiah, who comes, not to be rejected, but to reign.

> Rejoice greatly, O Daughter of Zion!
> Shout Daughter of Jerusalem!
> See, your king comes to you,
> righteous and having salvation,
> gentle and riding on a donkey,
> on a colt, the foal of a donkey (9:9).

Regarding what is known as the triumphal entry of Jesus into Jerusalem, Matthew (21:4-5) claims that this happened as a fulfillment of Zechariah's prophecy:

> "Say to the daughter of Zion,
> See your king comes to you,
> Gentle and riding on a donkey,
> on a colt, the foal of a donkey."

In Zechariah (11:12-13) prophesied the betrayal of Jesus for thirty pieces of silver.

> And I said unto them, "If you think good, give *me* my pay; and if not, keep it yourselves." So they weighed for my wages thirty *pieces* of silver. And the LORD said unto me, "Cast it to the potter: a goodly price" . . . And I took the thirty *pieces* of silver, and cast them to the potter in the house of the LORD.

Matthew, as he reflected in the role played by Judas, wrote in Matthew 27:3-7,

> Then Judas, who had betrayed him, when he saw that he was condemned, regretted it, and brought again the thirty pieces of silver to the chief priests and elders, Saying, I have sinned in that I have betrayed innocent blood. And they said, What *is that* to *us*? That's your problem. And he cast down the pieces of silver in the temple, and departed, and went and hanged

> himself. And the chief priests took the silver pieces, and said, It is not lawful for to put them into the treasury, because it is the price of blood. And they took counsel, and bought with them the potter's field, to bury strangers in. (KJV)

The prophet also prophesied the cleansing atonement of Christ's blood (cf. Zechariah 13:1 with John 1;29) and his passion: "They will look on me, the one they have pierced" (Zechariah 12:10).

Regarding the crucifixion, John wrote: "These things happened so that the Scripture would be fulfilled: 'Not one of his bones will be broken,' and, as another Scripture says, 'They will look on the one they have pierced'" (John 19:36-37).

Zechariah also prophesied: the conversion of Israel in the end times (cf. Zechariah 12:10-13:1, 9 with Romans 11:26); the destruction of the enemies of Israel (cf. Zechariah 14:3, 12-15 with Revelation 19:11-16); and the millennial reign of Christ (cf. Zechariah 14:9, 16 with Revelation 20: 4-6). So, it is quite evident that the New Testament authors believed in predictive prophecy. They saw in the Hebrew Scriptures the promises of Messiah and proclaimed Jesus as the fulfillment of the prophetic hope.

HOPE FOR THE FUTURE

Our secular prophets speak constantly of such issues as overpopulation, global food shortage, threat of nuclear war, epidemic outbreaks, economic recession, ecological disaster and terrorism. No wonder the suicide rate is so alarmingly high among our youth. Their tomorrows contain few rays of hope. Their prophets offer only darkness and gloom. Some will say, "But that's reality." No, it's not. Any prediction about the future that offers no hope is not reality. It merely contributes to the prevailing attitude of despair.

Reality is found in the truth of the Christian faith that proclaims that Jesus Christ will one day return. He will usher in a new age for his people at his second coming. This makes the task of Christian missions extremely urgent. We must win the lost. Every Christian ought to lead someone to Christ. My mother used to challenge me with this statement: "If everyone won one and every won-one won one, how many would be won!" We must issue a warning of judgment to come. But we must also joyfully exclaim the good news of brighter days ahead because our Lord is returning! Fasting will give way to feasting. This is not mere human optimism, for if God says there will be such a day; there will be such a day! Despair must give way to joyful dancing: "On that day a fountain will be opened to the house of David and the inhabitants of Jerusalem, to cleanse them from sin and iniquity" (Zachariah 13:1).

William Cowper appears to have been meditating on this when he wrote:

> There is a fountain filled with blood
> Drawn from Immanuel's veins,
> And sinner plunged beneath that flood
> Lose all their guilty stains.
>
> The dying thief rejoiced to see
> That fountain in his day;
> And there have I, as vile as he,
> Washed all my sins away.

There we all, as vile as he, may also wash all our sins away. The Christian faith proclaims that fountain was opened at Calvary. It is still opened today as the only sure remedy for the sins of the world.

The Old Testament prophets get much unnecessary and negative press because their message is often interpreted as harsh and intolerant. It is true that their righteous souls were often vexed about the prevailing sin and apathy in the society and among the people of God. However, careful reading will always reveal that special ray of hope, that special note of grace. The biblical prophets never leave us in despair. Zechariah's sincere and passionate pronouncements point to the coming of Messiah in whom future hope is embodied and through whom salvation is assured for the holy remnant that trust in his name and eagerly await his coming.

QUESTIONS FOR REFLECTION

1. What was the motive for Zechariah's call to return to the Lord?
2. What is the importance of the eight visions?
3. Why is it necessary to heed the word of the prophets?
4. What parts of Zechariah's prophecy give us hope for the future? Should Christians be optimistic about the future? Why?
5. Note the number of times "on that day" occurs. To what does this refer?
6. What prophecies of Zechariah were fulfilled by the coming of Jesus? What prophecies are still unfulfilled?
7. What does Zechariah consider to be the basic aspects of the religious life?

CHAPTER 12

MALACHI

The Prophet with Priorities

Malachi was the last of the post-exilic prophets and, indeed, the last of the Old Testament spokesmen for God. He ministered in the time of Nehemiah and condemned those sins which Nehemiah sought to correct. Malachi means "my messenger," and as the messenger of God, he directed his message against several specific sins: (1) the corruption in the priesthood; (2) the disregard of the Sabbath; (3) intermarriage with foreign women, that is, "daughters of a foreign god"; (4) the tolerance of social wrongs; and (5) the robbing of God by the neglect of the tithe principle.

THE FIRST MESSAGE (1:1-5)

The First message is an exhortation to respond to God's love. The people of God did not believe that they were loved by God. Malachi's theme throughout the whole book is that God loves his people. "I have loved you," and "I change not," says the Lord.

God's love is sovereign, unconditional, constant and personal. God declared his love for Israel in his sovereign choice of them as the way to bring Messiah into the world. He preferred Jacob over Esau for his purposes of continuing the messianic line. God's love for them was also a tough love. His punishment of Esau and Edom was to serve as a warning to his people as well as evidence of his love. The people of God should never doubt that they are loved. They should never pose such a sarcastic question as, "How have you loved us?"

THE SECOND MESSAGE (1:6-14)

The second message is a call to be genuine in their religious commitment. In this section we get some insight into the prophet's understanding of God. God is the one who makes himself known by three short statements (1:6, 14): one, "I am a father"; two, "I am a master"; and three, "I am a great king." The people, it seems, were not honoring, respecting or fearing him as father, master and king. In fact, the priests were despising his name and defiling the holy altar. They were offering defective sacrifices (the sick, the lame and the blind) and they were themselves unclean. Rather than setting a godly example of spiritual leadership, the priests were half-hearted, careless and indifferent. They were apparently unrepentant because they raised their hands in mock surprise at the charges laid against them by God through his messenger the prophet. "How have we despised your name? How have we defiled your altar?" they ask (1:6, 7). The corrupt leadership shrugged their shoulders and argued with God as if he were merely a junior employee criticizing management. From the passage it is clear that God would rather have no worship at all than false and insincere worship. God's people must be genuine in all aspects of worship and piety.

THE THIRD MESSAGE (2:1-16)

The third message is an invitation to love God with a single-heartedness of devotion. The priests did not love God with their whole heart, and by their lives they did not honor him. They failed in a number of important areas: (1) They failed to instruct the people in the true knowledge of God; (2) They failed to walk in the pathways of personal holiness; (3) They failed to evangelize, that it, to turn many from sin. Instead, the priests caused many to stumble and to turn from the way of truth. They violated the covenant God had made with their forefathers and did not remain true to the faith given them. Furthermore, they perverted justice in the courtrooms. In punishment, God says he will "curse" their blessings. He will spread "the offal" (dung) on their faces. It will be a drastic but needed lesson in humility. They will learn the lesson the hard way.

Their failure to love God with all their hearts is evident in the practice of mixed marriages. A cursory reading of this will support racial prejudice so we must not be naïve in interpretation. The Bible is not against racial intermarriage *per se*. Remember that Ruth from Moab was an ancestor of Jesus. In Malachi's time, there was a widespread "fad" of marrying the "daughter of a foreign god," that is, marrying someone outside the covenant family. Some commentators think this was a problem among the married Israelites! It was similar to the all too familiar problem of having an affair after one's wife has given birth to the children but now has lost her youthful attractiveness. In the quest for pleasure, many were dissolving their marriages by divorcing their wives. In such a culture, the women were being left destitute. No one "loves" divorce but, here, the major point is that God "hates" divorce. Why? God hated divorce because of what it did to people. Maybe it is because, in this particular context, divorce was being cruel to the woman. "A man covering himself with violence" (v. 16) refers to the cruelty of divorce. Malachi calls us to love God totally and to love the wife of our youth. The promises made in marriage are made to be kept. We must not break faith with our wives. C. S. Lewis once indicted that if marriage is based on sexual passion alone, it leaves no room for understanding marriage as a promise made. Our relationship with God is likened here to a marriage vow and unfaithfulness to God is seen as "spiritual" adultery. Therefore, God hates divorce but not divorced people. Let's be clear about that and not misuse Malachi.

THE FOURTH MESSAGE (2:17-3:12)

The fourth message is a call to trust the God who never changes. "I the Lord do not change," says God (3:6). That is the only reason why the people have not been totally destroyed by now. The blessings of salvation can be destroyed by sin, and the sinner can be excluded from the promises, but God ever remains faithful to his word. He will restore the penitent.

The people had wearied God with their questioning of his justice. They had made the terrible assumption that God was pleased with evil! How do we explain this? Maybe they saw the prosperity of their wicked neighbors in the light of their own poverty. Israel had rebuilt the temple, but they had not received the blessing prophesied by the earlier prophets. Therefore, they may have misunderstood their situation to mean that God was not just, or that he supported evil.

God made a promise to send a forerunner to prepare the way of the Lord, a messenger of the covenant who will come suddenly to the temple (3:1; 4:5-6). This was fulfilled by John the Baptist and the Lord Jesus. But it is possible that Malachi saw himself as the messenger, as should all Christians. We are messengers, whose job it is to deliver the message and then to be quickly forgotten. The message is always more important than the messenger. We are to be like John the Baptist who pointed to Christ, "Behold the lamb of God who takes away the sin of the world." "He must increase and I must decrease," he suggested. It is, after all, all about Jesus. It is not about us.

In chapter 3, verse 1, Malachi says, "The Lord whom you desire" will quickly come as a cleansing and purifying agent. I can't resist thinking that there is a bit of sarcasm here. They did not really "desire" him because, when he comes, he will refine and purge the people from their sin so that proper worship will be made. God threatened to be the accuser to lay charges against the sorcerers, liars, adulterers, and those who pervert justice and oppress the people. Before God could do his reviving work, he had to put his people through the refining fire. In the long run, there was nothing to fear, for like silver which is not destroyed by the flames but merely purified, God's people will be refined but not destroyed. The judging fires of God, for the believer, are meant to produce purity and holiness. They are not designed to destroy.

The fourth message also points out that God was being robbed of the tithe. There were several tithes required of the people, but every third year a tithe was to be brought to a huge storehouse in Jerusalem, a portion of which was to be distributed to the poor. Maybe the corrupt priests were misdirecting the portions of produce intended for the poor into their own pockets? We don't know. It is highly unlikely that God wanted his people to blindly give ten percent to corrupt priests. However, in this case to neglect the tithe was called robbery, and God specifically calls his people to return to him by returning to the tithe. Why? Was it because the corrupt leaders were being underpaid? No. The call for a return to the tithe came from God. The tithe was for the support of the priesthood, but it was also for the poor, the weak and the widow. What our modern taxes support today was part of the role played by the tithe. To make a simple demand across the board for a tithe today puts a heavy burden on the poor and modest income families. It is relatively easier for those in a higher income bracket.

However, the tithe is one tenth of our wages and profits from business or investments. Abraham paid tithes (Gen. 14:20). Jacob promised to tithe in gratitude to the Lord (Gen. 28:13-22). The use of the tithe ranged from underwriting the cost of a joyous religious feast in the sanctuary to buying "anything you wish" (Deut. 14: 22-29). Every third year the tithes stayed in the local vicinity and were used to support the priests, the foreigner, the fatherless and the widows (i.e., pastoral support and public welfare). The Levites lived on the tithe and also paid a tithe (Num. 18:26, Neh. 10:37-38). Tithing was specified as a way to "revere the Lord" (Deut. 14: 23). The tithe belonged God (Lev. 27:30) and to withhold it was to rob God (Mal.3:8). Prosperity is promised to the one who tithes (Mal. 3:10-12). When people stop worshipping God, the tithe is directed away from God's work (Amos 4:4). We support that which we value most. When God's people get renewed, among the first evidences of it is tithing (2 Chron. 31:5-12; Neh. 12:40-45).

In the New Testament, Jesus affirmed the principle of tithing (Matt. 5:17; Luke 11:42), but never established it as a legalistic obligation (Luke 21:3-4). The Pharisees boasted about it (Luke 18: 12; Matt. 23:23) while neglecting more important matters which they also ought to have done. Paul taught there was blessing in giving (Acts 20:35) and that it was for the work of the ministry (1 Cor. 9:14). All believers should regularly, proportionately, and cheerfully be involved in giving (1 Cor. 16:2-3; 2 Cor. 9:7). Make it honestly, spend it wisely and give it generously seem to be the Christian principles. Tithing is an ancient and honorable method of supporting the Lord's work. To modify it in any way is to dishonor the Lord and deprive ourselves of spiritual and material blessing (2 Cor. 9:6). It can be neglected only to the detriment of God's work and the loss of personal blessing.

Tithing ought not to be blindly demanded as a legalistic rule that oppresses people or excludes them from fellowship. Full disclosure of how the tithe is spent ought to be the rule not the exception in our financial statements. Some religious groups demand tithes of people who should actually be recipients of it. In earlier times, if one didn't tithe one could have one's ears cut off! Yes, the tithe has been used as a weapon of oppression but it has, just as often, been abandoned. The Lord, in this prophecy, informs the people that obedience to the tithe would result in a blessing for which there would not be room to contain. The floodgates of heaven would open, that is, rain for the crops and vines would produce an abundant harvest. There is a challenge to test God in this matter so that the surrounding nations would take notice.

THE FIFTH MESSAGE (3:13-4:6)

The fifth and final message in Malachi is a challenge to take an inventory. This is a recurring theme in the prophets. The shallowness of the people's religious experience is evident in the question, "What do we get by serving the Lord?" (3:14). It appears that their only motive for serving God was for what they got out of it. As far as they could see, there was more immediate profit in being evil. For all intents and purposes, the arrogant were the real "blessed" of God. So, why serve God?

But there is always the faithful remnant that fears the Lord. Those who made up this remnant talked about true worship and honored God's name. It is this remnant that will be God's treasured possession when the day of the Lord comes. Their names are written in a book of remembrance. God will not forget them, though the world despises them. They are the jewels of God, his beloved ones. They will survive the great day of the Lord, but the wicked will be consumed. The fire of judgment, like a furnace, will destroy the unrighteous, but for the righteous the fire will be the Sun of righteousness. The people of God will rejoice on that day like a calf let loose from the barn on a bright summer's afternoon. Let us take an inventory to see if we are among this remnant.

Malachi exhorts us to remember God's law and he ends his book with a prophecy of an "Elijah" who will come in the last days before the final day of the Lord and by whose ministry a great ingathering will take place. From this prophet the church can be assured of God's love in the light of which we are called to be genuine and sincere. We are called to respond to his love with a dedication that is whole-hearted. We are called to trust and obey the God who never changes. We are called to take inventory lest our names not be in the book of remembrance on that day when God makes up his treasured possession.

QUESTIONS FOR REFLECTION

1. What references to Malachi are made in the New Testament?
2. What is Malachi's doctrine of God? Example: He believes God is a loving God (1:2).
3. What are the duties of a priest, according to Malachi? Compare Malachi 2:7 with Romans 15:16.
4. How does Malachi deal with the divorce issue? Is his view compatible with the New Testament's teaching?
5. Is Malachi's comment about tithing still relevant today? Are there other scriptures on tithing that ought to inform our understanding of this practice?

CHAPTER 13

Toward a Revival of Biblical Preaching

Some people find preaching to be the most boring and useless part of Christian worship. Why? Several reasons are usually given: the dogmatic stance of the pastor on every possible issue; the lack of any forum to question the content of the sermon; the unfamiliar theological language; and the apparent lack of preparation on the pastor's part which results in constant repetition of two or three themes making every sermon sound alike.

In some pulpit presentations, which pass for sermons, the Scripture passage read resembles the singing of "O Canada" before a hockey game. It gets the proceedings off to a good start but has little if anything to do with what comes after the opening face-off.

Preaching needs to be revitalized today because the mass media is dominating the attention of our congregations. The challenge before the evangelical ministry is to make preaching more effective.

In this multimedia age, the evangelical preacher faces the alluring temptation to play to the gallery, to use secular techniques of motivation, manipulation and marketing to keep the crowds and offerings coming. The financial responsibilities of bigger and better church buildings place unimaginable strain upon the pulpit as a vehicle of fund-raising. The ever-increasing surfacing of personal, psychological and family problems in the average congregation forces many of us to play amateur "expert" delivering "How to do it" messages which are gathered more from popular books than from Scripture. We rationalize, "New day, new problems, new methods." As a result, our preaching can become anthropocentric rather than Christocentric. In our eagerness to be relevant, is it possible that we may be contributing to a famine for the Word of God? Is it not possible that the "church-hopping" which is so evident today may be a symptom of a real hunger for the Word?

Is there any need for prophetic preachers who proclaim a biblical message? Has their place been supplanted by the multitude of gospel gurus, religious entertainers, and ready made messages available on the audiocassette, videotape, satellite dish, DVDs, and downloaded PowerPoint presentations? Do we need people in the pulpit who are men and women who hear from God and are faithful to his Word? Has prophetic biblical preaching run its course? Can preaching meet the needs of evangelical churches today?

WHAT BIBLICAL PREACHING IS NOT

What I am calling prophetic biblical preaching is not merely cultural analysis and commentary. Often called "topical" preaching, this form of presentation is quite inspiring and informative, but it lacks the solid authority of a "thus saith the Lord." Many "topical" preachers endeavor to be biblical and prophetic. However, far too many topical sermons are based more on the "opinion" and "personal preferences" (often disguised as convictions) of the speaker than on genuine exegesis of Holy Scripture. This is quite evident when the topic centers around music or standards of outward piety. We must be careful of always appealing to "principles" and "convictions" without giving a clear explanation of how we arrived at those "principles" and "convictions."

Prophetic biblical preaching is not a scholarly lecture on theology. The pulpit is no place to make an ostentatious display of learning. Learning must be servant to truth. It must be employed in the service of proclamation. It exists merely to serve. No preacher should consider himself qualified to preach unless he is master of his books. Likewise, he should avoid the pulpit until he is mastered by the Book. It is the Book that must be declared in the pulpit, not the books. Plain preaching is the rule of thumb. Words that hide the truth rather than make it known should not be uttered from the pulpit. True prophetic preaching is not an exhibition, but an exposition. It is a laying out in full visibility, before the hearers, the Word of divine truth. It is a displaying of the cross before the eyes of the people.

Prophetic biblical preaching is more than a harsh condemnation of the prevailing attitudes in our culture. Some self-proclaimed "prophets" appear to delight in the negative message appealing to already held prejudices of their audience. For others, their "forte" is shearing the sheep, not feeding them. Only pastoral love legitimizes prophetic license. A prophetic voice which speaks from a heart lacking compassion surely falls short of the biblical precedents. No pastor ought to adopt a prophetic posture in the pulpit unless he has earned that right by loving his people.

Prophetic biblical preaching is not "popular" psychotherapy. In the Middle Ages, the confessional had a more important place than the pulpit. In some parts of the evangelical church, pastoral counseling is in danger of becoming the Protestant confessional, with all the attendant dangers. Pastoral counseling is a needed ministry. I do not wish to be misunderstood. Pastoral theology can be enriched by a wide spectrum of sources. However, the preacher's role in the pulpit is not to use the weapons of the world. We do not fight using secular weapons, but with spiritual weapons of the Word, the Spirit, prayer and Christian compassion. It is sad to see an imbalance in evangelical Bible colleges and seminaries, where there are several courses offered in the field of psychology and counseling, but rarely any in the areas of prayer and spiritual disciplines.

The "pop" psychology available in many Christian bookstores must not replace the good news of Christ in evangelical pulpits. Subjects such as "How to Raise Teenagers," "How to Have a Happy Marriage," "How to Get over Depression," etc., have a place in the overall teaching ministry of the church. Their place, however, is secondary to the proclamation of the gospel by an anointed preacher. When preaching takes second place to the lecture or the screen, the church is in danger. When the pulpit is used to proclaim personal opinions, preferences and experiences rather than the clear Word of God, the pulpit is no more than any other public podium. The pulpit should be reserved and revered as the sacred platform for telling forth of the good news of the gospel of God's saving grace.

Prophetic biblical preaching is not social activism. Liberalism of bygone days proclaimed a utopian kingdom without the coming King. It is ironic that some evangelicals seem to support similar concepts. The pulpit is not a place to inspire people to vote for a cause, but to bring them face to face with the truth of God. Social activism can easily become another form of works-righteousness. Preachers should not be champions of political causes or social movements, but proclaimers of the "faith once delivered."

Some evangelical social reform groups sound strangely postmillennial in their theology. Some socially active Christians seem willing to reject the view that the church is a "called out" company of last-day believers. Some are adopting a new doctrine of the church where eschatology finds little place in their preaching.

Let us not forget, rightly or wrongly, the traditional motive for missions and holiness among most evangelical Christians in this country was influenced by our hope for the soon return of Christ. Time was short, we used to preach, and therefore we must win the lost. Christ is coming for his prepared bride, we used to preach, and therefore let us cast off worldly pleasures and be ready. Placing priority on this life at the expense of the next is spiritual disaster for evangelical believers.

Neither is prophetic biblical preaching social isolationism. The tension between this and the previous point may be a difficult one to resolve. However, remaining silent in the face of social evils will surely bring the judgment of God upon the church. Our positions must not be nebulous, but clear. Preaching that does not sound a definite alarm against sin, personal and corporate, is surely not biblical preaching.

Prophetic biblical preaching is not party-line preaching. An overemphasis on "distinctives" may certainly establish one's denominational orthodoxy, but it hardly represents the "whole counsel of God." A survey of one pulpit, done by the author, revealed that out of twelve sermons, eight were on the second coming, three on baptism in the Holy Spirit, and one on divine healing. The pastor was not preaching on a series; he had simply fallen into the habit of preaching on favorite topics. Many of the messages were filled with camp-meeting cliches, and proof texts. Although this author had no quarrel with the theology, it seemed like the same message over and over again with a different text. The presentation was inspiring, with great doses of side-splitting humor. The presentation was enjoyable, but I came away feeling I have been to a theatrical pep rally and not to an explication of God's holy Word. To preach a "full" gospel, one needs to declare not only the distinctives of our faith, but the whole of it.

Why is there a lack of prophetic biblical preaching? Is it possible that the fear of theological education has kept us from being students of the Word? Has the anti-intellectualism which has plagued evangelicalism for decades backfired? Has our fear of education made us biblical illiterates? Or has our preoccupation with "books" kept us away from the Book? Has it produced spiritual incompetence because we are not saturated with the only source for biblical preaching? Can we experience a revival of biblical preaching in our day?

WHAT PROPHETIC BIBLICAL PREACHING IS

Prophetic biblical preaching is expository preaching. It is declaring or speaking out the good news. The good news is God-centered, not man-centered. Such preaching is an explanation of the text in order to make Christ known. It is preaching that uses illustrations as windows into the text, not as distractions from the text.

Prophetic biblical preaching is a proclamation of the message of the cross. It is a message of redemption to a world which needs, not exhortation, but conversion. The good news of justification by faith in Christ's blood is still at the heart of the gospel.

Prophetic biblical preaching is doctrinally sound. Such a preacher will heed the admonition of Paul, "Take heed unto thyself and unto the doctrine; continue in them; for in doing this thou shalt save thyself and them that hear thee" (1 Tim. 4:16, KJV). Some Christians are blown about by every wind because many sermons are weak in doctrinal content. Can we be truly prophetic and biblical without being doctrinal?

Prophetic biblical preaching is passionate preaching. It is a serious business. It is not for the half-hearted, but for those intent on being channels for the Lord's use. The greatest encouragement to preach prophetically and biblically is the fact that the Holy Spirit graciously accompanies the preaching of the Word. The anointing of the Holy Spirit creates a fire in the bones and burning in the heart. This results in a presentation that is convincing and convicting. Nothing can substitute for that special touch. All our preparation is merely loaves and fishes which are too few for so many, unless the Spirit of the Holy One comes down.

Prophetic biblical preaching includes a call to holy living. The preacher must also model the Word as well as preach the Word. If life and speech are not in harmony, the message will be unheeded and reproached. The preacher's life must not become divorced from the preaching. Preaching becomes ineffective if the preachers are careless with their lives. Preachers are also sheep as well as shepherds. What they preach they must practice. Our character must reflect Christ-likeness. Moral purity and personal uprightness must be the constant companions of biblical preaching

In Acts 6:2-6 we are told the serving of the tables distracted the apostles from their basic work of preaching the Word of God. Their main duty was to be distributors of divine truth, ministers if the Word. Paul advised Timothy, "Preach the Word" (2 Tim. 4:2). This was to be Timothy's all-encompassing purpose in his ministry.

Prophetic biblical preaching is still God's way of confronting us with himself. Prophetic biblical preaching is a priority. It is the most effective way to convince unbelievers of their need, to exalt the Lord Jesus Christ and to encourage holiness of life. If we are to be anything, evangelicals must be prophetic and biblical. We must be people of the Book. Once more we need to wait upon God in prayer and meditation, on bended knees, before its open pages. Let us pray for a new anointing of the Holy Spirit. We must let the Bible speak from our pulpits. Let all other voices be silent.

Books For Further Reading

The following list is merely a sampling of the rich treasures available in any theological library. However, I have found these authors particularly stimulating and helpful. I highly recommend them for the serious student or pastor.

Achtemeier, Elizabeth. *Minor Prophets I.* NIBC Peabody: Hendrickson, 1996.

Baldwin, Joyce G. *Haggai, Zechariah, Malachi.* Downers Grove, Ill.: InterVarsity Press, 1972.

Boice, James M. *The Minor Prophets.* 2 Vol., Grand Rapids: Michigan: Zondervan, 1983.

DiGangi, Mariano. *Twelve Prophets.* SP Publications, 1985.

Feinberg, Charles. *The Minor Prophets.* Chicago: Moody press, 1976.

Kaiser, Walter, Jr., *Malachi: God's Unchanging Love.* Grand Rapids, Michigan: Baker Book House, 1984.

Kaiser, Walter, Jr., *Toward an Old Testament Theology.* Grand Rapids, Michigan: Zondervan, 1978.

Kidner, Derek. *The Message of Hosea.* Downers Grove, Ill.: InterVarsity Press, 1981.

McConville, J. Gordon. *Exploring the Old Testament: A Guide to the Prophets.* Downers Grove, Ill.: InterVarsity Press, 2002.

Motyer, J. A. *The Message of Amos.* Downers Grove, Ill.: InterVarsity Press, 1974.

Robinson, George. *The 12 Minor Prophets.* Grand Rapids, Michigan: Baker Book House, 1978.

Stuart, Douglas. *Hosea-Jonah.* WBC. Waco: Word Books, 1987.

Printed in the United States
19353LVS00005B/486